HOW TO J
FIELD E\

by Mike Parmiter

© British Athletic Federation
225A Bristol Road, Birmingham B5 7UB

First edition	(Dr. S.E.J. Best)	1957
Second edition	(V.C. Sealy)	1965
Third edition	(Revised by C.A. Sinfield)	1969
Fourth edition	(C.A. Sinfield)	1976
Fifth edition	(M.W. Parmiter)	1989
This edition	(M.W. Parmiter)	1996

ISBN 0 85134 139 X   1.5K/18.5K/08.96

Designed and printed in England on 115gsm Fineblade Cartridge by Reedprint Ltd, Windsor, Berkshire SL4 5JL.

CONTENTS

ABOUT THE AUTHOR

Mike Parmiter recently retired from Kings Langley School in Hertfordshire, having held the position of Head of the Technology Faculty and also Head of 6th Form.

He took up judging in 1959 whilst a member of Aldershot, Farnham and District Athletic Club. Although a qualified official at both track and field, it was in field judging that his experience developed, officiating at Club and County level while he was in Hampshire.

In 1970 he moved to Hertfordshire and since then has represented the County on the South of England AA General Committee, has been a member of the SEAA Officials Committee for a number of years and is currently the Hertfordshire Officials Secretary. He is Vice President of the Dacorum and Tring Athletic Club.

An experienced official at all levels of the sport, Mike Parmiter became a Field Referee in 1980. He has officiated regularly, either as Field Referee or Judge, at Area, National and International meetings over a number of years. He has Refereed the European Club Championships on two occasions, was Clerk of the Course at the European Junior Championships, and was appointed an Athletics Technical Official at the XIII Commonwealth Games in Edinburgh. He officiated at the European Indoor Championships and the World Student Games in 1991, was appointed Technical Manager for the IAAF Grand Prix Final in 1993, and was Referee — Jumps for the IAAF World Cup in 1994.

PREFACE

The aim of this book is to raise the standard and quality of judging at all levels of competition. Whatever the experience of the official — from the interested lay person to the seasoned international — it is hoped that it will be of benefit in developing a deeper knowledge and understanding of judging. Indeed, it should be helpful to everyone wishing to widen their interest in athletics, whether as an official, competitor, spectator or armchair athlete.

Since the last edition of this publication there have been a number of changes, both with regard to rules and to the inevitable refining of judging techniques. Substantial revision of the text has therefore been necessary and the addition of extra material should be of benefit to newer officials.

All Diagrams and Photographs supplied by Mike Parmiter.

INTRODUCTION — JUDGING FIELD EVENTS

Athletics is probably the most popular of all participation sports. The simple desire to run faster, jump or throw further or jump higher than others has gripped all ages for centuries. Whether it is just to gain satisfaction through a personal sense of achievement or simply to be better than others, it is probably true that most people have taken part, at one time or another, in some form of athletic competition.

As competition levels increased, rules were introduced to give each competitor an equal opportunity to compete fairly. Then, as these rules were established and refined, so judges were needed to control the competitions and to see that the rules were adhered to in a fair manner.

The beauty of the sport is that, even today, regardless of the level of competition — be it School, Club, Area, National or International — it still maintains its simplistic approach. The rules are the same for all and the duties of the judges are still to see that fair competition prevails at all times.

The judging of field events requires officials to have a thorough knowledge of eight different disciplines, four jumps and four throws, and while there is some overlapping of the rules from one event to another, each discipline develops its own characteristics. In fact there are over thirty different duties involved in judging the complete range of field events. It is important for officials to widen their experience by undertaking as many different duties as possible. For example, the official who enjoys the long jump and at most meetings judges that event, could be somewhat thrown if asked, say, to judge pole plant and adjust stands in the pole vault.

Besides having a sound knowledge of the rules and a wide spectrum of experience, it is also important for officials to understand the needs and moods of competitors. Often, the usually placid athlete becomes edgy and aggressive before and during a competition. A firm but pleasant approach will be necessary to defuse a situation that not only could create tension between athlete and official, but could also be off-putting to the other athletes in the competition.

Being able to handle athletes, regardless of their reputation, is an important factor when judging. In competition all athletes are of equal standing and no one competitor should be allowed to get away with "stretching a rule". This is tantamount to gaining an unfair advantage over the other competitors. Whether it is exceeding the time allowed for a trial, trying to take more than the permitted number of warm-up trials, incorrect use of check marks or receiving any form of assistance, the official must be firm and totally impartial in the interpretation of the rules. The confidence and respect of all the competitors will be gained by a competent and fair official and the event will be better for it.

Judging field events demands a great deal of concentration from all officials. The temptation to glance round at an exciting track race or to let one's mind wander must be resisted at all times. Not only could it be a potentially dangerous situation when an implement is being thrown, but accuracy in measuring can easily be lost as well. Likewise, resist the temptation to talk to the competitors during an event, except for checking numbers and calling them up for a trial. Obviously if they talk to you, you should answer them; but once the event is over the atmosphere is more relaxed, and the athletes generally appreciate it when an official compliments them on a good competition or performance.

Field judges also have an input which goes beyond actual judging. Some ground staff, although keen on their job and very conscientious in their general maintenance, lack the athletic background which would make them aware of the many small details required, particularly in field events. This is where the competent official can help in seeing that these extra facilities are provided, making things better for athletes and judges alike and hopefully raising the standards of the stadium for the future.

On a wet day, for example, throwers will need some means of drying and cleaning their implements without having to use their own track suits or towels. Stadiums can often be persuaded to keep a supply of cloths for such occasions. The provision of mats and brooms at throwing circles is essential to enable athletes to wipe their feet before entering the circle. A clean, dry surface will give a much better foothold. Benches or seats on which athletes can sit while waiting their turn are most useful. They not only provide relief from standing between trials for the competitors, but also allow a clearer view of the events for all spectators.

The popularity of athletics, particularly through an increase in televised meetings, has inevitably led to higher standards of presentation and general meeting organisation. It is normal practice now for graded officials to wear navy or black blazers, ties and grey trousers/skirts when judging. Indeed at all major and most indoor promotions judges are usually requested to wear white trousers/skirts and white shirts or blouses with their blazers. The image and appearance of officials is just as important to the overall presentation of a meeting as it is to see that the athletes are dressed correctly. It is also accepted practice for officials to refrain from smoking within the arena and whilst judging.

Throughout this book the rules for competition and relevant specifications have been taken from the current British Athletic Federation (BAF) publication *Rules for Competition,* effective from 1st April, 1996. While it is safe to assume that the majority of rules will remain constant over a number of years, readers are reminded that the International Amateur Athletic Federation (IAAF) — the world governing body — and BAF regularly monitor all rules and specifications. It is therefore recommended that officials update their rulebooks regularly and note all changes and amendments.

DUTIES OF OFFICIALS

THE FIELD REFEREE

The duties of a Field Referee are to:

1) Take control of all field events.

2) Allocate judges to particular events and duties.

3) Check that equipment and markings conform to specific rules.

4) Announce to judges and ensure that the competitors are informed of the number of trials and the appropriate starting heights to be allowed under the relevant rules, even if this is printed in the programme.

5) Ensure that the events start on time.

6) Supervise the measurement of performances.

7) Check the final results.

8) Decide in the event of any difference of opinion between the field judges — the Referee's decision shall be final.

9) Deal with any disputed point as provided by the rules.

If there is to be a number of field events, the duties can be shared or sub-divided by more than one Referee. It is normal practice, for example, at larger meetings to appoint a Referee for jumps and a Referee for throws. It may also be desirable for separate Referees to be appointed at Combined Events for Decathlon, Heptathlon and Pentathlon.

If more than one Referee is appointed, it is important that they work closely together, both before and during the meeting. It is often a useful tip for one of the Referees to produce a combined duties sheet as one person can have an overview of the whole timetable and can deploy the officials accordingly. The judges are much more likely to get a varied spread of duties as a result.

The Referee's duties will invariably start well before the day of the meeting. Every effort should be made to obtain a copy of the programme and timetable and also the names and grades of all the appointed judges from the Meeting Organiser well in advance — although this is not always possible.

The Preparation of Duties Sheets

When allocating duties, it is clear at the outset that a number of factors must be taken into consideration. The standard of the meeting, the number of officials available, their competence and experience, the timetable, safety considerations, etc, must all be considered.

At major meetings all judges will be extremely experienced — usually Grade 1's and Referees. It will still be necessary to choose the right mix of officials for each judging team. The choice of team leaders, the desire to give the judges balanced and varied duties whenever possible, must also be considered.

At other meetings, however, there will be many occasions when the Referee will have to allocate duties amongst judges of a wide range of experience, right down to the willing ungraded helper. The main consideration, however, for any Referee must be the smooth, efficient and safe running of the meeting.

The preparation of duties sheets must be done with care. By looking through the competition rules for each event, it is clear that there are a number of duties that must be included in order to comply with the rules. Other duties are necessary to help with the smooth running of the event.

Throughout this book each of the eight field events has a typical allocation of duties included, together with a simple sketch showing the approximate positions of the judges required to carry out the duties. These will, of course, vary depending on the number of officials available.

If there is a shortage of judges for a meeting it is important that the essential duties are covered by experienced officials, whenever possible, in all events. For example, if only two graded officials are available in a throwing event, make sure that one is at the circle and the other is out in the field. In this way they will be able to keep an eye on the other less experienced judges. An example of a preliminary strategy for producing a duties sheet is given at the back of the book together with a sample sheet.

Whenever possible, try to let all officials have their duties lists before the date of the meeting. This will enable them to take the necessary equipment with them to carry out their tasks and also permit the less experienced officials to go over their duties before the meeting. If it is not possible to send out duties sheets in advance, they should be available to be given out as the officials arrive.

There will be times, however, when the Referee will not know who his judges are until shortly before the meeting is due to commence. A useful tip is to have a duties list drawn up to meet the requirements of the programme but excluding the actual names of the judges. As the judges report in they can be assigned to duties and their name can be entered in the appropriate spaces on the sheet. If insufficient judges are available, which is quite likely to be the situation at some minor meetings, it may be necessary to appeal to the spectators for help with some of the less technical tasks.

The Day of the Meeting

It is very important that the Referee arrives at the stadium well before the start of the first event to check out the facilities and equipment being used. Never assume that everything will be in perfect condition. All markings and sector lines must be checked for accuracy. Ground staff are not infallible and even at major stadiums it has been necessary to correct errors in the markings. It can be quite frustrating and annoying if, after a record has been broken, it is subsequently invalidated because of inaccuracies in the markings, particularly if by a simple check before the meeting it would have been noticed and put right.

All Referees should be safety conscious and must always inspect take-off boards, landing areas and safety cages before the start of a meeting. The high jump and pole vault stands must be checked to see that they are in working order, and the verniers must be set and taped so that they are not accidently altered.

Even if a Technical Officer is appointed — as is usual at major meetings — the Referee is still entirely responsible for all field events. He must therefore satisfy himself that all the throwing implements conform to the specifications laid down in the rules. It will be necessary to weigh and measure all shot, discoi, javelins and hammers to be used in competition and to mark them in a distinctive way. The use of coloured adhesive tape or a waterproof marker pen are both satisfactory methods. Whatever system is used, it must be clearly identifiable to the judges of the event. They must see that only those implements approved for competition are actually used.

If an athlete wishes to use his or her own implement — subject to the rules of the competition — it must be submitted to the Referee for approval before the start of the competition. It must not automatically be assumed that an implement approved at a previous meeting is still acceptable for competition. This is not necessarily so. A useful tip is for the Referee to initial and date his mark and, if necessary, remove all other marks.

It is necessary to see that the judges have everything required to run their events efficiently: rakes, brushes, tapes, crossbars, etc. These tasks would be carried out by a Clerk of the Course, under the Referee's control, if one is appointed. When EDM (Electronic Digital Measurement) is used, the Referee must be satisfied that it has been set up correctly and the officials are conversant with its operation.

If it is at all possible, a short briefing session with the judges before the meeting starts is often quite useful. It is a good way of passing collectively to the judges any special information regarding the meeting: starting heights, number of trials, arrangements for getting athletes to presentation, safety, procedure for records, etc.

During the Meeting

Once the meeting is under way, the Referee must move around the competition sites supervising events and checking measurements. It is important to observe all the officials in a team during a competition. This is best done in an unobtrusive way. It can sometimes be quite inhibiting and off-putting to have the Referee breathing down one's neck in the middle of a competition. A quiet word is all that is necessary to speed up an event or to correct a judging technique.

The Referee must personally supervise the checking of all records and see that the appropriate record application form is filled in correctly. It saves time and trouble if Referees carry a supply of record forms around with them. (These are available from the BAF office). At the end of each competition the result cards must be checked and signed before they are recorded and announced.

The Referee is in a unique position at an athletics meeting — a position that must not be taken lightly. By good, sound preparation it is possible to anticipate and resolve potential problems so that the field events programme can flow smoothly, to the benefit of athletes and judges alike.

FIELD JUDGES

The duties of Field Judges are:

1) To see that the field events are carried out in accordance with the rules.

2) Decide the order in which the competitors shall be placed.

In jumping for distance separate judges shall be responsible for:

1) Deciding if the take-off is fair.

2) Marking the point in the landing area from which the measurement is to be made.

3) Recording the wind speed for the designated period of time.

In jumping for height two judges should keep a record of the jumps and check their recordings at the end of each round. The height of the bar should be measured when the bar is raised, particularly when standards or records are being attempted.

In throwing for distance separate judges shall be responsible for:

1) Deciding if the delivery is fair.

2) Marking the point of landing of the implement from which the measurement is to be made.

Before the start of each event the judges should ensure that the right competitors are present, that they are correctly dressed and are wearing numbers as on the programme.

All field judges come under the direct control of the Field Referee. They should carry out all duties assigned to them to the best of their abilities. To do this, judges must have a sound knowledge of the rules for competition and must interpret them fairly. On occasions the intention of the rule may need to be taken into consideration when arriving at a proper decision. If a judge has any doubt about a particular jump or throw, the athlete must always be given the benefit of that doubt.

The need to arrive early at a meeting cannot be over-emphasised. Good preparation is the essence of good judging and this cannot be so if, at the last minute, officials are running around looking for essential equipment for their event. Athletes warm up to reach a peak at the scheduled time of starting. Delays, for whatever reason, can be very frustrating and detrimental to the competition. Never assume that all the facilities will be available and in perfect condition for the start of competition. All officials should arrive sufficiently early to carry out the necessary checks on the events they have been allocated to. For most events at least half an hour is essential to carry out these tasks, although for high jump and pole vault a minimum of one hour is more realistic as the stands and verniers must be set before the athletes arrive for warm up.

It is normal practice for the Referee, in planning his duties list, to allocate an event leader for each of the competitions. Whenever possible this will be an official of reasonable experience, and this judge should be responsible for seeing that the event proceeds smoothly according to the rules. The event leader should see that any special instructions issued by the Referee concerning the event are carried out.

The judges must see that the competition areas are clear of all people not involved with the events. Whether they are coaches, parents, friends or just spectators, they must all be well away from the event sites. For events inside the arena this means they should be outside the track as, apart from safety implications, any form of coaching or assistance within the arena could possibly result in disqualification of the competitor. When events take place outside the track, it is useful to arrange for a roped off area specifically for spectators.

The judges should see that the implements approved for competition are accessible to competitors, preferably on a stand or rack. It is a requirement, subject to regulations laid down by the Promoting Body, that any competitors wishing to use their own implements must submit them to the Referee for approval. Under BAF rules, an athlete shall not use another's implement without the owner's permission. However, with the exception of vaulting poles, this does not apply to meetings held under IAAF rules when all implements must go into a general pool and be made available to all competitors.

All non-approved implements must be cleared from the event site before the start of the competition.

Order of Trials

The order of trials is usually decided by a draw prior to the commencement of the competition. In jumping or throwing for distance, it is normal practice for competitors to take their trials in the order stated on the card. The judges can, however, change this order if circumstances warrant it. For example, if an athlete is competing in more than one event taking place at the same time, the judges can allow a trial to be taken out of order within the appropriate round, enabling the competitor to get to the other event. However, no competitor is permitted to take more than one trial in any one round, so that if a trial is missed and the round is completed, that trial cannot be subsequently taken.

COMPLETING A RESULTS CARD

One of the most important duties for field judges is keeping the event card. It is the only official record of all the distances jumped or thrown by the competitors so a meticulous standard of recording is necessary. If two cards are kept in any competition they must be compared regularly, particularly at the end of each round and when completing the result.

Before the event starts a check must be made to see that the number, name and club of each competitor is recorded correctly. The athletes must be told the order of competing and any details concerning number of trials, starting heights and subsequent height progression.

Distances or trials must be recorded clearly. Remember, after the event the cards often have to be photocopied and results circulated to many different sources. Incorrect recording of results due to indecipherable cards can be annoying and frustrating. The use of a black ball pen is preferred for recording as it photocopies well and does not run when wet. Never leave a blank space. If a trial is not taken, a dash (–) must be put in the appropriate place. A no throw or a no jump should be recorded as NT or NJ respectively.

In jumping or throwing for distance, it helps to underline the best trial for each competitor and bring it forward to the appropriate column. If the best six or eight competitors are to go forward for three extra trials, it is important that the positions after the first three rounds are accurately worked out and checked against the second card. A line can be put through the spaces for trials 4 to 6 for all competitors who do not qualify to go forward. This prevents accidently calling them by mistake. At the conclusion of the competition, bring forward the best performance for each competitor and record these in the best of all trials column. The final positions can then be worked out and be confirmed against the second card and by the rest of the judging team.

If the best performances of two or more competitors are equal then the tie must be resolved accordingly. See the section below regarding the resolving of ties.

Once the judges have decided the correct order of finishing the number, name, club and best performance for each competitor must be entered in the result section at the foot of the card. It is not normally necessary for the judges to award points at this stage; this is usually done when the cards are sent in to the recorders.

At a league match, however, it will be necessary for the judges to decide the result in the light of 'A' strings and 'B' strings when this system is in operation. In normal league competition each club is represented by two competitors. Regardless of the initial position on the card, the competitor with the final best performance for each club automatically becomes the 'A' string and the other the 'B' string. Therefore, when working out the result, first go through each club and designate who is 'A' string and who is 'B' string. The final placings can then be decided amongst the 'A' strings followed by the 'B' strings. The result is then recorded in separate columns in the appropriate section.

After the result is completed the card must be checked and signed by all the event judges. It is finally given to the Referee, who will check that the card is accurate, confirm the result and then sign the card as correct.

If an application for a record is to be made in any field event, the grades of the officials judging the event must be added to the card.

RESOLVING TIES

Jumping or Vaulting for Height

Ties shall be decided as follows:

(a) The competitor with the lowest number of jumps/vaults at the height at which the tie occurs shall be awarded the higher place.

(b) If the tie still remains the competitor with the lowest number of failures throughout the competition up to and including the height last cleared shall be awarded the higher place.

(c) If the tie still remains:

(i) if it concerns first place, the competitors tying shall have one more jump/vault at the lowest height at which any of them finally failed, and if no decision is reached the bar shall be lowered or raised 2cm for High Jump and 5cm for Pole Vault. They shall attempt one trial at each height until one competitor clears a height and the remaining competitor(s) fail at the same height. Competitors so tying must jump/vault on each occasion when resolving a tie.

(ii) If the tie concerns any other place other than first, the competitors shall be awarded the same place in the competition.

Jumping or Throwing for Distance

In the case of a tie, the second best performance of the competitors tying shall determine the result. If the tie remains the third best trial will be decisive and so on.

If the tie still remains:

(i) If it concerns first place, the competitors so tying shall have such additional extra trials as are necessary to resolve the tie.

(ii) If the tie concerns any other place, the competitors shall be awarded the same place in the competition.

TECHNICAL MANAGER

It is normal practice to appoint a Technical Manager for all major meetings, whether they are held under BAF or IAAF rules.

This is a senior appointment and the official will have the total responsibility for ensuring that the track, runways, circles, arcs, safety cages, landing areas for field events and all other equipment are in accordance with the relevant rules.

He or she will:

(a) check and verify that all implements conform to specifications of weight, size and material;

(b) ascertain that windgauges, timeclocks, photofinish and EDM are set up and in working order;

(c) check high jump and vaulting stands are in good order — at some meetings TMs may also have to check hurdles and starting blocks;

(d) check that all safety sector ropes are in place.

When Technical Managers are appointed they shall have sole responsibility for the duties of the Clerks of the Course and will allocate their duties accordingly. The Referees will undertake this duty if no TM is appointed. These duties have been explained in the Clerk of the Course section.

When checking implements look at the requirements of the rules:

SHOT — Weight, diameter, is it round? check several times, is the surface smooth? are there flats or indentations to give extra grip?

DISCUS — Weight, diameter — including the centre plate, thickness, rim and surface — are they smooth? symmetry, flatness of sides.

HAMMER — Weight, diameter of head, centre of gravity, length, damaged wire, handle, spindle — worn or seized?

JAVELIN — Weight, length, grip, centre of gravity, specifications to tip and to tail, metal head — size, is it loose? smooth surface.

Remember: all throwing implements issued for competition should exceed the specified weights by at least 5gms.

When adjusting take-off boards, check for stability and linear movement. Are they level with the ground? Does the plasticine indicator fit correctly? To adjust unstable boards, there are four adjusting bolts set underneath on each corner with locking nuts attached. Loosen the locking nuts and adjust the bolts until the board is flush with the ground. This is usually achieved by trial and error. Once this is done, re-tighten the locking nuts to prevent further movement. Be prepared for rusty nuts and bolts! Always have easing oil and spanners handy.

It is clear that the Technical Manager will be an official of considerable experience with a good understanding of the overall organization of an athletic meeting, and it is with this official that the Meeting Manager, TV, etc, work closely to make certain all is set up as required.

CLERK OF THE COURSE — FIELD

The Clerk of the Course, under the jurisdiction of the Technical Manager or the Field Referee, is responsible for seeing that all facilities are ready for the conduct of a meeting. It is vital to see that all the markings and circles are correct as required by the rules; that take off boards and stop boards are clean and firmly positioned; plasticine indicators are prepared and all landing areas are safe and ready to use. Throwing cages and areas must be checked for safety and that the gates on the hammer cage operate correctly.

To maintain competition sites in a fit state, all auxiliary equipment — brooms, rakes, rollers, etc, must be available as required and judges be provided with marking spikes and measuring equipment as necessary.

If a Technical or Equipment Officer is not appointed the Clerk of the Course is responsible for the weighing and issue of implements for both practice and competition. It is important to see that they are removed from the site of the event as soon as the event is completed.

This is an extremely important appointment at any athletics meeting, requiring a good understanding of the demands of all field events including specifications for implements. It is so easy to overlook the valuable contributions made by a

SPECIMEN HEIGHT CARD

HEIGHT SCORE CARD

Event	SENIOR LADIES HIGH JUMP
Date	10-7-95
Event No.	12
Time	12.15
Venue	WARNERS END
Meeting	HORSHIRE COUNTY CHAMPS
Standard	
Record(s)	1.74 m

Competition Order	Competitor's Number	Name	Club	Starting Height	1.45	1.50	1.55	1.60	1.63	1.66	1.69	1.72	(Metres)	Best Performance (Metres)	Trials at Height Cleared	Total Failures	Final Position
1	16	C. BOWLES	LANGLEY A.C.	1.50	—	0	0	X X 0	X X 0	X X X				1.63	2	3	4 =
2	22	K. JOHNSON	ABBOTTS A.C.	1.55		—	0	X X X						1.55			7
3	6	C. PATON	CONISTON A.C.	1.45	X 0	X X 0	X X X							1.60			6
4	15	J. CONGLETON	POTTON A.C.	1.450	0	— T 0	0	0	X X 0	X X X				1.63	2	3	4 =
5	31	C. PRICE	WARNER AC	1.450	0	0	X 0	X X 0	0	X X 0	X X X			1.66	2	3	3
6	3	K. GERRARD	LEA HARRIERS	1.50		0	0	0	0	0	X X 0	X X X		1.69	1		1
7	19	S. GROVE	APSLEY & DIST.	1.50		— X	0	0	0	X 0	X — X			1.66	1		2
8																	
9																	
10																	
11																	
12																	
13																	
14																	
15																	
16																	

Legend:
- — = jump not taken
- X = failure
- 0 = valid jump

Handwritten annotations:
- record starting heights
- fill in number, name and club
- complete result
- total trials at height cleared then total failures to resolve ties
- time fault
- jump off for 1st place only
- 3 successive failures regardless of height
- sign card

RESULT

Place	Number	Name	Club	Metres	Points
1st	3	K. GERRARD	LEA HARRIERS	1.69	
2nd	19	S. GROVE	APSLEY & DIST.	1.66	
3rd	31	C. PRICE	WARNER A.C.	1.66	
4th	16	C. BOWLES	LANGLEY AC	1.63	
4th	15	J. CONGLETON	POTTON A.C.	1.63	
6th	6	C. PATON	CONISTON AC	1.60	
7th	22	K. JOHNSON	ABBOTTS AC	1.55	
8th					

(4th = 4th tied)

RESULT (B)

Place	Name	Club	Number	Points	Metres	Points
(1st) 9th						
(2nd) 10th						
(3rd) 11th						
(4th) 12th						
(5th) 13th						
(6th) 14th						
(7th) 15th						
(8th) 16th						

Judges: P. Jones, J. Jackson, K. Smith

Referee: R. Palmer

SPECIMEN DISTANCE CARD

DISTANCE SCORE CARD

Event	SENIOR MEN — JAVELIN
Date	10-7-95
Event No.	16
Time	14.30
Venue	WARNERS END
Standard	
Record(s)	
Meeting	HORSHIRE COUNTY CHAMPS — 62.24 m

Competition Order	Competitor's Number	Name	Club	FIRST trial Metres	SECOND trial Metres	THIRD trial Metres	Best of three trials Metres	Position after three trials	FOURTH trial Metres	FIFTH trial Metres	SIXTH trial Metres	BEST of all trials Metres	Final Position
1	9	D. SIM	APSLEY & DIST	52.64	54.72	49.16	54.72	5	N T	51.16	53.86	54.72	6
2	18	M. JOINER	ABBOTTS A.C.	N T	49.32	50.08	50.08	8	(52.18)		49.32	50.08	8
3	27	B. KENDALL	LEA HARRIERS	49.18	51.00	52.10	52.10	6	55.64	56.42	49.32	56.42	5
4	20	P. REDDING	WARNER A.C.	45.62	47.36	51.78	51.78	7				51.78	7
5	2	A. PARROTT	LANGLEY A.C.	N T	N T	56.42	56.42	4		N T	(56.08)	56.42	4
6	13	C. McMAHON	POTTON A.C.	N T	58.18	---	58.18	2	59.94	N T	61.42	61.42	3
7	10	B. RANDALL	HART A.C.	60.04	61.42	58.74	61.42	1	60.76	62.22	59.26	62.22	1
8	24	S. ALLEN	CONISTON A.C.	57.74	55.90	52.60	57.74	3	N T	61.98	N T	61.98	2
9	33	M. SMITH	GADE A.C.		38.44	49.32	49.32	9				49.32	9
10													
11													
12													
13													
14													
15													
16													

Annotations (handwritten):
- fill in number, name and club
- throw not taken
- complete result
- underline and bring forward best trial
- no throw
- best 6 or 8 — 3 further trials
- sign card
- javelin, discus, hammer — all measurements to the nearest even centimetre below distance thrown
- next best resolves tie

Judges: A. Browne, 1 C&X, G Scott, W. Vincent, J. Moore
Referee: R. Palmer

RESULT

Place	Number	Name	Club	Metres	Points
1st	10	B. RANDALL	HART A.C.	62.22	
2nd	24	S. ALLEN	CONISTON A.C.	61.98	
3rd	13	C. McMAHON	POTTON A.C.	61.42	
4th	2	A. PARROTT	LANGLEY A.C.	56.42	
5th	27	B. KENDALL	LEA HARRIERS	56.42	
6th	9	D. SIM	APSLEY & DIST.	54.72	
7th	20	P. REDDING	WARNER A.C.	51.78	
8th	18	M. JOINER	ABBOTTS A.C.	50.08	

RESULT (B)

Place	Number	Name	Club	Metres	Points
(1st) 9th	33	M. SMITH	GADE A.C.	49.32	
(2nd) 10th					
(3rd) 11th					
(4th) 12th					
(5th) 13th					
(6th) 14th					
(7th) 15th					
(8th) 16th					

STACY REF 193

9

C of C when events are running smoothly and to remember that it was necessary to arrive several hours before the start to prepare the stadium.

The position of Clerk of the Course is an arduous task and one that should not be taken lightly.

To carry out the wide range of duties associated with this position, close co-operation will also be necessary with the ground staff. A knowledge of the stadium is a great advantage and for an important meeting it is often desirable to make a visit beforehand to check the facilities. This gives time for any faults or deficiencies to be corrected before the day of the meeting.

Regardless of whether you are familiar with a stadium or not you can never guarantee that all equipment will be in perfect condition. It is therefore necessary to have access to a few handy tools on the day, such as pliers, spanners, screwdrivers, scissors, penknife, etc. Coloured tapes and calipers for marking and checking implements, chalk, wedges for stabilizing take off boards — all are useful.

It is good practice to prepare a check list of tasks to be done and equipment to assemble for each event. It is so easy to overlook even the most obvious item on occasions, but with the help of a list each item and event can be checked off as it is dealt with.

WIND GAUGE OPERATOR

This is increasingly becoming a common duty to be undertaken at both Long Jump and Triple Jump events. At one time it was quite rare to see a wind gauge in use at any meeting other than major championships, but as more stadiums acquire the equipment, it is now familiar at most League, County and Inter-Area matches as well. It is a requirement that the details of the wind speed must be measured and recorded before a record claim can be submitted in these events.

A wind gauge consists of a cylindrical tube fitted with a suitably designed set of fan blades. The stronger the wind the faster the blades turn. The wind speed is recorded in metres per second on a digital read-out on the front of the gauge. It will record whether it is a following wind (a plus reading) or a head wind (a minus reading). An example of a wind gauge is shown below.

The gauge must be set up not more than 2 metres from the edge of the runway and parallel to it. It must be positioned 20 metres from the take-off board and at a height of 1.22 metres.

The velocity shall be measured for a period of 5 seconds from the time a competitor passes a mark placed 40 metres in Long Jump or 35 metres in Triple Jump from the take-off line. If a

Using a wind gauge

A CHECK LIST FOR CLERK OF THE COURSE — FIELD

POLE VAULT

Stands in good working order
Safe landing area
Bars
Firm, clean box
Runway markers
Scoreboard
Time clock and windsock
Measuring device
Red and white flags
Stadium vaulting poles if available
Vaulting pole rack

HIGH JUMP

Stands in good working order
Safe landing area
Bars
Run-up markers or coloured tape
Brush or squeegee
Scoreboard
Time clock and windsock
Measuring device
Red and white flags
Steps or chair

LONG JUMP

Well dug pit
Firm take-off board
No-jump indicator(s)
Roller or trowel
Rakes and brushes
Measuring tape and spike
Scoreboard
Time clock and windsock
Runway markers
Wind gauge
Water and can
Distance markers (side of pit)
Red and white flags

TRIPLE JUMP

Well dug pit
Firm take-off board(s)
No-jump indicator(s)
Roller and trowel
Rakes and brushes
Measuring tape and spike
Scoreboard
Time clock and windsock
Runway markers
Wind gauge
Water and can
Distance markers (side of pit)
Red and white flags

SHOT

Check circle and extension lines
Stop-board
40° sector lines and flags
Safety ropes
Brush and mat
Measuring tape and spike
Absorbant cloths
Correct weight shots
Implement stand
Red and white flags
Time clock
Scoreboard
Calcium carbonate powder

HAMMER

Check circle and extension lines
40° sector lines and flags
Safety sector, cage, gates
Distance markers
Brush and mat
Measuring tape and spike
Absorbant cloths
Correct weight hammers
Implement stand
Red and white flags
Time clock
Scoreboard
Warning horn

DISCUS

Check circle and extension lines
40° sector lines and flags
Safety cage and sector ropes
Distance markers
Brush and mat
100m measuring tape and spike
Correct weight discoi
Implement stand
Absorbant cloths
Red and white flags
Time clock
Scoreboard
Warning horn

JAVELIN

Check runway and extension lines
Arc and 8m centre
Safety ropes
Sector lines and flags
Distance markers
Correct weight javelins
Implement stand
Absorbant cloths
100m measuring tape and spike
Time clock
Scoreboard
Warning horn
2 sets of red and white flags
Runway markers

competitor runs less than this, then the reading shall be taken from the time the competitor commences the run.

When recording the wind speed, it shall be rounded to the next higher tenth of a metre per second in the positive direction. (For example: a reading of +2.03 m/sec shall be recorded as +2.1 m/sec; whilst a reading of –2.03 m/sec shall be recorded as –2.0 m/sec. If there is no wind it shall be recorded as zero (0). Do not leave a blank.

Wind gauges tend to be battery operated and this is activated manually by a switch which automatically switches off and locks the reading after the required 5 seconds. Although the recording card will be the same as those recording distances jumped, the wind gauge operator will only record wind speeds after each trial.

The maximum permitted following wind speed for the acceptance of a record is +2.0 metres per second. In Combined Event competitions the wind speed shall not invalidate a record unless it exceeds 4.0 metres per second.

This duty is often combined with operating a time clock or call up. Care must be taken not to stand in line with the wind gauge, thus preventing a smooth flow of air through the cylinder. This will clearly give a false reading. A red light is usually situated on the gauge to denote that the battery is failing. It is a useful tip to check the battery before the start of the competition.

GENERAL CONDITIONS FOR ALL FIELD EVENTS

There are a number of conditions within the rules for competition that apply to all athletes. It is not the intention to reproduce the rule book here but to highlight these conditions in general terms. Over a period of time rules tend to be modified or added to in order to reflect changing attitudes and thoughts and it is recommended that the current rule book is consulted to get the appropriate definitive rule(s). It is important to point out that there are some subtle differences between the BAF and IAAF rule books. It is desirable, therefore, to have access to both current rule books, particularly for those likely to be called upon to officiate at meetings under both codes.

Clothing

In all events competitors must wear at least vest and shorts, or equivalent clothing, which are clean and so designed and worn as not to be objectionable even when wet.

Unless the Referee has given permission for a change to be made, all competitors competing in a team event must wear the registered colours of the team they are representing.

Footwear

Competitors may compete in bare feet or with footwear on one or both feet. As footwear is permitted in order to give stability, protection and a firm grip on the ground, shoes must not incorporate hidden springs or other such devices to give the athlete additional assistance.

The sole and heel of the shoes may be constructed to provide for the use of up to 11 spikes and an athlete may use any number up to 11. When a competition is held on a synthetic surface the length of spike that projects from the sole must not exceed 9mm, with the exception of High Jump and Javelin events where it must not exceed 12mm. For non-synthetic surfaces the maximum length of spike shall be 25mm with a maximum diameter of 4mm.

Numbers

Competitors shall be supplied with two number cards corresponding to their number in the programme or entry list. They must be visibly worn as issued and not be cut, folded or mutilated in any way. The numbers must be displayed, one on the back and one on the breast. Competitors in the High Jump and Pole Vault may wear one number only, either on the back or the breast.

If competitors wish to take their field event trials wearing their tracksuit or other covering, they must wear their numbers on the outside so that they are clearly visible.

Advertising

Limited advertising on athletes' clothing is permitted. In principle, the accepted name of an affiliated club can be displayed on vests and tracksuits in letters no more than 4cm high. Club sponsorship advertising is permitted, but must be submitted to the British Athletic Federation for approval. Sponsorship details may also appear on number cards, but these are also subjected to size restrictions.

Recording of Measurements

In Long Jump, Triple Jump, High Jump, Pole Vault and Shot Putt all measurements shall be recorded to the nearest 1cm below the distance or height measured if that measurement is not a whole centimetre. That means all fractions of a centimetre are to be ignored.

In Discus, Hammer and Javelin events measurements are recorded to the nearest EVEN centimetre below the distance thrown.

Assistance

Athletes must not receive advice or assistance during a competition from anyone within the competition area. It is good practice, therefore, for the judges to clear the competition site of all those not actually competing before starting the competition. It is not an offence to receive advice or encouragement shouted from outside the arena. The athlctes, however, must not leave the competition site in order to seek advice.

A wind sock may be placed near the take off in all jumping events to show the direction and strength of the wind.

Under IAAF rules the use of cassette recorders, radios or similar devices is not permitted. Although this rule does not apply to competitions under BAF rules, it is strongly recommended that the use of them is discouraged for safety reasons.

Draws and Trials

In all competitions a draw shall be made to determine the order of competition. It is possible for the judges to alter this order if necessary. For example, if an athlete is entered in more than one event taking place at the same time, the trials may be taken in an order different to the pre-determined draw. However, when this happens, competitors throwing or jumping for distance are not permitted to hold over any of their trials to a subsequent round or have more than one trial recorded in any one round.

In jumping or vaulting for height, although athletes are allowed up to three trials at any one height, they also have the option to jump at their discretion. This allows them not only to pass a height if they so wish, but having failed once or twice at a particular height, to take their second or third trial at a subsequent height.

Three successive failures, regardless of height, disqualifies from further participation — except, or course, in the case of a jump off. Once a competitor declares an intention to pass a height, the athlete cannot subsequently take an attempt at that height.

Delay

The length of time not normally to be exceeded for taking a trial is $1^1/_2$ minutes for all events with the exception of the Pole Vault when 2 minutes are allowed. These times are taken from the moment when everything is ready for the trial to begin. In the final stages of a High Jump or Pole Vault competition, when 3 or fewer athletes remain, the time shall be increased to 3 minutes for HJ and 4 minutes for PV.

For competitions held under IAAF rules, when only one competitor is left, the time is increased to 5 minutes for HJ and 6 minutes for PV. The time for consecutive trials by the same athlete shall be 3 minutes for HJ and 4 minutes for PV.

It is recommended that a time clock be set up to indicate the countdown to the competitors in all events.

Qualifying Rounds

When the number of competitors is too large to allow a competition to be conducted satisfactorily, a qualifying round may be held. Qualifying heights or distances shall be set by the organisers and the competitors shall be divided into two or more groups or pools of roughly equal numbers. Unless there is the facility to hold each group at the same time and under the same conditions, each group shall start the competition immediately the previous group has finished.

Apart from High Jump and Pole Vault, each competitor shall be allowed up to three trials. Once a competitor has reached the qualifying standard, he or she shall not continue in the qualifying competition.

If fewer than 12 competitors reach the qualifying standard, the numbers for the final shall be made up to 12 by taking the next best performances.

A time clock and windsock

DEPLOYMENT OF JUDGES

When judging an event officials will usually be deployed by the Referee as part of a team. Some events will require more officials than others, but it is desirable to maintain at least a minimum number for the efficiency and safety of each event. There will be many occasions, however, when even the minimum number is not available. Clearly there will be times when one or two judges will have to run an event almost single handedly with, perhaps, some assistance from the competitors or spectators — to pull a tape through, replace bars or return implements, etc. This contrasts very much with an international or televised meeting when the number of officials is often increased to accommodate the extra demands placed on the judging teams.

It is the intention of this book to indicate the basic requirements for each event appropriate for an average meeting. Simple diagrams are also given to indicate the suggested positions for the judges to carry out their duties. A possible strategy for the preparation of a complete duties list is given towards the end of the book.

For ease of reference the eight field events have been divided into three sections:

a) Jumping for Distance –
   Long Jump and Triple Jump.

b) Jumping for Height –
   High Jump and Pole Vault.

c) Throwing Events –
   Shot Put, Hammer, Discus and Javelin.

Inevitably, there will be some overlap with judging duties across events but the intention has been to cover, in general terms, each discipline as comprehensively as possible without the need for too much cross referencing.

JUMPING FOR DISTANCE

LONG JUMP

Duties of Officials

Judge 1 – Leader, card 1, take-off board, flags, measure, check scoreboard.

Judge 2 – Card 2, take-off board, pull tape through, repair no-jump indicator.

Judge 3 – Pit judge, spike, zero end of tape, exit from landing area.

Judge 4 – Call up, runway control, check marks, time lapse, check numbers and spikes, (windgauge).

Judge 5 – Pit judge, rake.

Deployment of Officials and Duties for Long Jump

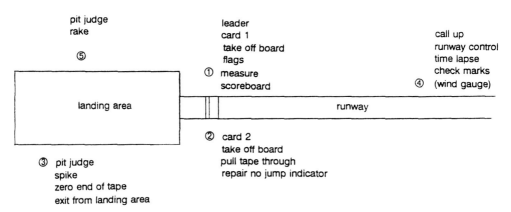

Safety Considerations and Preparation before the Start

The judges should first satisfy themselves that the facilities conform to the specifications laid down in the current BAF rules. Is the run up safe and the take-off board firmly fixed down and flush with the ground? A wobbly board can cause an athlete to twist an ankle on take off or to land awkwardly, thus causing an injury. Most take-off boards are interchangeable, particularly those on synthetic surfaces, and can be lifted out of their recesses by two hooks. Simple adjustments to the screwed feet can alleviate rocking and raise or lower a board that isn't flush. While on this point, during the winter months or after heavy rain these recesses often fill with water and can cause quite a problem with water splashing out each time an athlete takes off. This can cause the take off area to become very wet and slippery and an un-expected hazard is created.

The sand in the landing area — is it level with the take-off board and sufficiently moist to give a clear impression to measure from? Compacted sand is very hard to land on and can cause jarring to an athlete. It is important to dig the pit and loosen the sand well before the start of the com-petition. It is also useful to have a watering can handy during competition, particularly on very hot days.

Most stadia have plasticine no-jump indicator boards now. Check that more than one is avail-able to fit the board and the plasticine is pliable enough to take a clear mark. It speeds the com-petition up if an indicator, marked by a no jump, is immediately replaced. It can then be repaired without delaying the event. A wallpaper seam roller is most useful for removing marks on the plasticine. If a plasticine no-jump indicator is not available, it will be necessary to bank up moist sand to the required specification immediately beyond the take-off board.

The judges should check that there is a spike and tape for measuring purposes, a rake for levelling the sand and a brush to keep the board clean. Make certain the rake and spike are not left

A Valid Jump

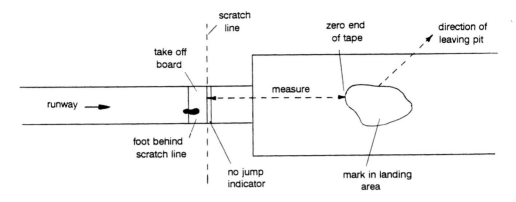

in positions that can cause possible accidents. If it is necessary to put either of them down between jumps, keep them well away from the landing area and, in particular, never leave the rake with the prongs facing upwards.

Jumping runways are often sited in front of the main stand. It certainly gives maximum spectator coverage which is excellent for the event, but it does often increase the number of people who, for various reasons, need to cross the runway. Be ever vigilant for this. Apart from being off putting for the athlete, a collision at speed can be extremely serious.

At higher graded meetings the use of a scoreboard, time clock and wind gauge is normal practice. Where these are used, they must be checked to see they are sited correctly and are in working order.

Apart from setting up the event, it is also necessary to supervise the warm up before the competition starts. Many athletes arrive early to measure out their run up and to place check marks to assist their jumps. Check marks are not permitted on the runway itself, so the judges must watch to see that marks do not mysteriously appear, e.g. that talcum powder does not accidently get knocked over on the runway!

Judging the Event

Judge 1 will be responsible for the smooth running of the event. This official should be positioned on the extended scratch line with a clear view of the take-off board and no jump indicator. It is a foul jump if an athlete touches the ground beyond the scratch line or scratch line extended in an attempt — whether jumping or not. This will

be recorded on the card with NJ by the athlete's trial, and signalled with a clear call and by raising a red flag. Due to the slight curve at the front of some shoes, it is possible for an athlete with long spikes to have a toe marginally projecting over the scratch line without actually touching the ground or the indicator. If the judge, however, is satisfied that the athlete has not touched the ground beyond the scratch line, a valid trial must be given and a white flag raised.

Judge 1 will also be responsible for reading the measurements and recording them onto the card. The distances shall be recorded to the nearest centimetre below the distance covered, i.e. fractions of a centimetre must be ignored. After a jump has been recorded, the judge should stand on the runway until the pit has been levelled and is ready for the next competitor.

Judge 2 should be positioned on the other side of the take-off board from Judge 1. After a valid jump, this official will be responsible for holding the tape at right angles to the scratch line to enable Judge 1 to read the measurement. The measurement should also be recorded on card 2 as a check. The duties will also include changing and repairing the no-jump indicator should a no-jump be given.

Judge 3 is the pit judge and will be responsible for marking the break in the sand nearest to the scratch line from where the measurement is to be made. The judge should have a spike and the zero end of the tape to undertake this task (see the section on measuring). It is also important to watch for any infringements in the landing area that could invalidate the trial.

The break in the sand refers to that made by the athlete in the course of landing. It need not necessarily be made by the feet; it could be hand, foot, seat or any other part of the anatomy. For example, if an athlete lands and steps back to maintain balance, or puts a hand behind to stop falling backwards, it is from the nearest break in the sand to the scratch line that the measurement is taken. However, if in the course of landing a competitor touches the ground outside the landing area nearer to the scratch line than the mark in the pit from which the measurement would have been taken, it shall not be measured but recorded as a no-jump. For example, an athlete lands in an unstable position and puts a hand outside the landing area behind his landing point to prevent himself falling backwards. If his hand had been behind him in the landing area the measurement would have been taken from that point. It is against the spirit of the rule and is therefore not permitted.

This is particularly relevant on a dual purpose pit where an extra wide landing area accommodates both long and triple jump. With such a large area of sand to jump into, it would be difficult for the pit judge to interpret this rule satisfactorily. Therefore, to define the extent of the landing area, a tape or rope must be positioned through the pit to give the required landing area and centralize the runway. Effectively this makes the area beyond the tape outside the landing area for that particular event.

Once a jump has taken place, do wait until the athlete has left the landing area before moving in to spike and measure. The judge should note that the competitor should leave the pit in a forward motion. It shall be recorded as a no-jump if, after landing, the athlete walks back through the pit. Effectively he or she is making a mark successively nearer to the scratch line with each step taken. Athletes usually use this method of invalidating a trial when they are dissatisfied with the jump and do not wish it to be measured. This gives rise to an interesting point. When is a jump completed? If an athlete, having had a valid take off and left the pit correctly, subsequently decides that he doesn't wish to have the jump measured, can he re-enter the landing area to invalidate the jump? It is generally accepted that once an athlete has left the pit the jump is completed. It must therefore be measured and recorded.

If a competitor makes more than one impression in the sand and the pit judge has difficulty in deciding which mark is nearer to the scratch line, he should not hesitate to tell the judge at the board that he would like more than one measurement taken. It can sometimes be quite deceptive, when marks are well apart, as to which is closest to the scratch line. A request to 'take two' has been made by most judges at some time or another. When this happens the shorter distance of the two will be recorded.

The pit judge, apart from spiking, should also be responsible for supervising the levelling of the sand in the landing area. At smaller meetings where there is a shortage of officials it is likely that the raking will also form part of his duties. Mention has already been made of the importance of level and moist sand to give an accurate measurement. It is so critical that the result of the competition could depend on the quality of the levelling. Several centimetres could be lost or gained by careless raking. Where possible, particularly at major meetings, it is desirable to use experienced officials to carry out this task rather than rely on inexperienced lay people. Good rakers will also speed up a competition.

The most usual way to level the sand is with a rake, but occasionally large scrapers are used. These certainly level the sand well but are heavy to operate and are quite time consuming, prolonging the event considerably.

There is a tendency to play down duties such as

Centralizing a Combined Landing Area

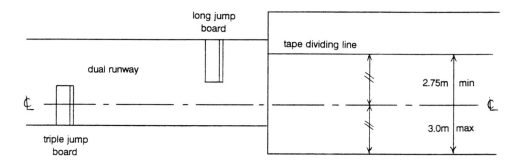

Importance of Level Sand in Long and Triple Jump Landing Areas

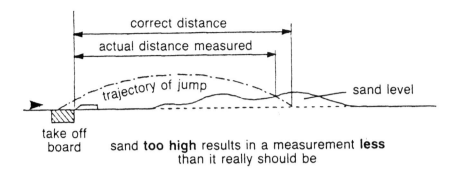

sand too high results in a measurement **less** than it really should be

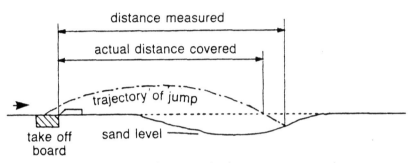

sand too low results in a measurement **further** than it really should be

pit raking, assuming that they are inferior and secondary tasks. Remember that all duties are of equal importance and each have their part to play in providing an efficient and well run competition.

Judge 4 will be responsible for calling up the athletes and keeping the competition moving. It is recommended that this task is best done by operating down the runway in contact with the competitors. The judge will be in the ideal position to check that each competitor is wearing the correct number front and back, and that these are as issued and not mutilated or folded in any way. During warm up, while checking that the athletes are present, the official can also check that their shoes are fitted with the correct number and length of spikes.

It is recommended that when a judge calls an athlete to take a trial, the next one or two are also called to get ready. For example, "Number 4 to jump, followed by numbers 6 and then 2" enables the latter two to complete their preparations so they are ready to jump when called.

Each athlete should be called once the landing

area is level and the officials at the jumping end are ready. From the moment they are called (not from when they take their track suit off) each competitor has 1½ minutes to complete the trial. If a time clock is in operation it should be set up in full view of the athlete on the runway. If a visual time clock is not available, it is useful to have a watch handy and let the athlete know when, say, there are 15 seconds remaining of the trial.

Although the call up judge will have a copy of the event card, it is not necessary to record on it the distances jumped by each competitor. A tick on the card when the competitor has jumped is all that is required, as the measurements will be recorded by the officials at the board. If an athlete, however, jumps out of order or misses a trial for any reason, the judge must make certain that this information is relayed to the judges at the take-off board.

When fewer officials are available to judge the event, the call up judge could be dispensed with and his duties done by Judge 1 at the take-off board.

Long and Triple Jump Landing Area

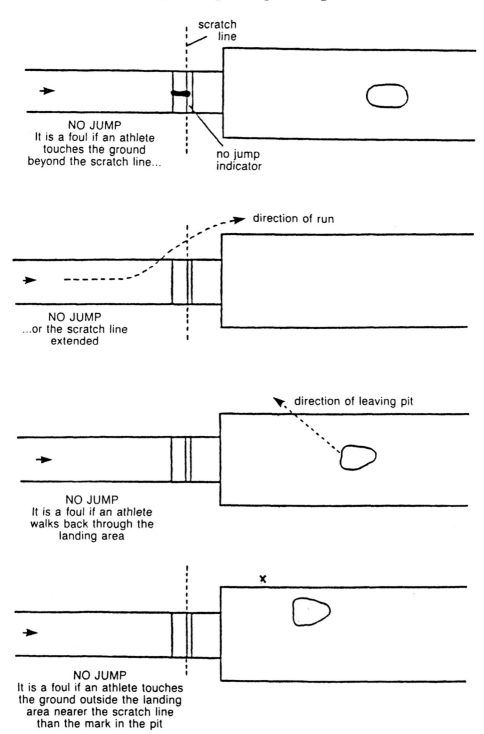

scratch line

NO JUMP
It is a foul if an athlete touches the ground beyond the scratch line...

no jump indicator

direction of run

NO JUMP
...or the scratch line extended

direction of leaving pit

NO JUMP
It is a foul if an athlete walks back through the landing area

x

NO JUMP
It is a foul if an athlete touches the ground outside the landing area nearer the scratch line than the mark in the pit

TRIPLE JUMP

Duties of Officials

Judge 1 – Leader, card 1, take-off board, flags, measure, check scoreboard.

Judge 2 – Card 2, take-off board, pull tape through, repair no-jump indicator.

Judge 3 – Pit judge, spike, zero end of tape, exit from landing area.

Judge 4 – Call up, runway control, check marks, time lapse, check numbers and spikes, (windgauge).

Judge 5 – Jump sequence, rake pit.

Deployment of Officials and Duties for Triple Jump

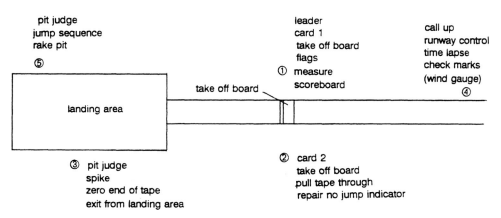

Judging the Event

Effectively, everything that has been written about the Long Jump applies to the Triple Jump with the exception of the jump sequence. The hop shall be made so that competitors land on the same foot with which they have taken off; in the step they shall land on the other foot, and the sequence is completed with a jump into the landing area. At one time it was recorded as a failure if the trailing or 'sleeping' leg made contact with the ground during the sequence. This no longer applies. Provided the hop, step and jump are carried out in the correct order, any contact with the ground with the trailing leg is ignored.

The judge appointed to watch the jump sequence should stand in a position that gives a clear uninterrupted view of the jump. The most favoured positions are either (i) by the side of the landing area — where a head on view of the athlete is obtained, or (ii) from behind the take-off board where the judge will have a receding view of the competitor. Either position is suitable and also enables the official to see that the hop and step phases are within the runway. They have

the added advantage that the duty can be combined with other essential tasks, so reducing the number of officials required for the event. At the landing area the sequence can be observed either by the judge appointed to spike the landing or to rake the pit. In the other position, behind the take off, the duty can be combined with pulling the tape through or repairing the no jump indicator.

When an athlete uses a hitch kick style, it can be somewhat confusing to the inexperienced official to decide whether the sequence has been completed in the correct order. For a jumper who takes off with the left foot, the sequence is left, left, right before going into the jump phase. It will be reversed for a right-footed take off.

The rule is quite specific regarding measuring, i.e. from the nearest break in the landing area. Therefore if an athlete fails to reach the landing area, or if the nearest mark to the scratch line from which a measurement would have been made is on the runway, it shall not be counted as a valid trial but recorded as a no-jump.

There are several choices of take-off board available for athletes to suit their performance.

Sequence for Triple Jump

HOP must take off and
land on same foot

STEP must land on
opposite foot

JUMP must land in
the landing area

These are usually 9m and 11m from the landing area for women and junior men and 11m and 13m for senior men. It will be found, however, that fluctuations will occur from the recommendations depending on the level of competition. For boys and girls who are developing their skills, it is often necessary to improvise and make a temporary board with whitewash or tape at, say, 7m or 8m if they cannot reach the landing area from the shortest existing board. If this happens, note the take-off requirements of each athlete before the start of the competition. It is useful to write this information by their names on the card so that the take-off judge can be positioned by the appropriate scratch line. If different take-off boards are used in the same competition, remember to move the no-jump indicator accordingly and to put blanking strips in the spaces at the other boards for safety.

The question of when to call a no-jump in Triple Jump often arises. To call out 'no-jump' immediately after take off may cause the athlete to pull up suddenly and cause injury. Marginal fouls, however, can only be discovered at the completion of the jump by studying the no-jump indicator. It is recommended, therefore, that to be consistent and fair to all competitors, a no-jump should be signalled at the end of the sequence by raising a red flag.

At the end of the competition the judges should place the competitors in the correct order of finishing, complete the result section and sign the card before giving it to the Referee for checking. This is standard practice for all events.

A scoreboard

JUMPING FOR HEIGHT

HIGH JUMP

Duties of Officials

Judge 1 – Leader, card 1, call up, height progression, control runway and check marks, check spikes and numbers, check measure.

Judge 2 – Card 2, set bar, measure, validity of jump, take-off, check scoreboard.

Judge 3 – Set bar, measure, plane of uprights, time lapses, flags, supervise warm up.

Deployment of Officials and Duties for High Jump

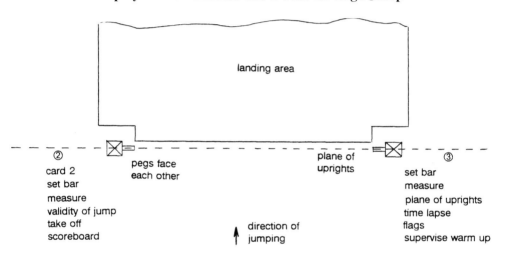

Safety Considerations and Preparation before the Start

It is essential for the officials to assemble early at the event site to satisfy themselves that everything necessary to conduct the event is at hand. Uprights in good working order, spare bars, adhesive tape for check marks, a time clock and a measuring device. Although it is true to say that all eight field events are specialised disciplines in their own right, high jumpers and pole vaulters tend to arrive quite early to sort out their run-ups and familiarise themselves with the facilities and conditions. It is important that all preparations for the event are carried out in sufficient time before the start of the competition — preferably before the athletes arrive, although this is not always possible. Accidents can easily occur if athletes are trying to sort out their run-ups while the officials are still setting the uprights and verniers.

It is crucial that the landing areas are safe to land on. Clear specifications are laid down in the rules regarding size and thickness and these must be strictly adhered to. High jump and pole vault beds are usually made up of sections for ease of movement and storage. It is important that these sections are firmly fixed together to ensure there are no gaps for the athletes to fall through on landing.

Landing beds are usually positioned on wooden pallets to assist drainage and reduce foam deterioration. For safety reasons, these pallets must not protrude beyond the landing area.

In wet weather it is often necessary to sweep away puddles and surface water from around the take-off area. This is the area that gets the most wear and a wet, worn surface is likely to be very slippery under these conditions.

Setting the Bar

1. Place the uprights in a stable position with the measurements facing outwards (away from the landing area). Check that the pegs supporting the bar are facing each other. There should be a clearance of at least 1cm between the bar and uprights to prevent the bar being jammed on. The uprights should be so positioned that there is a clearance of 10cms between the plane of the uprights and the landing area.

2. When the officials are satisfied with the position of the uprights, mark round the base with adhesive tape or chalk. If the uprights are moved or knocked over during competition, this will ensure they are replaced in exactly the same place each time.

3. Set the supporting pegs to a predetermined height, say 1.50m, and check with either a measuring device or tape that they are level at each end. Adjust as necessary.

4. Set the competition bar on the pegs. If the bar appears straight or with only a small uniform deflection, measure the height at the centre of the upper surface of the bar perpendicular to the ground. If the bar appears to sag or there is uneven deflection, measurement must be made at the point where it is lowest. This need not necessarily be at the centre. Once the measurement has been taken, set the verniers on the uprights to this height. Now take another check at a different height. It is a good idea to take a check somewhere around the height that the competitors will start jumping. When the judges are satisfied that the verniers are set correctly, tape over the

Supporting Pegs for High Jump

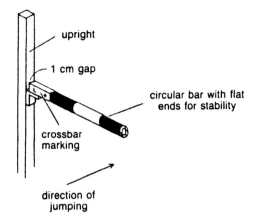

upright

1 cm gap

circular bar with flat ends for stability

crossbar marking

direction of jumping

locking screws so that they cannot be altered during competition. It is also important to mark the ends of the bar distinctly so that it can be replaced in the same way throughout the competition.

Whenever possible, use a rigid measuring device to check the heights. A flexible tape is fine in an emergency, but tends to bend even in the slightest breeze and accuracy could be lost. It would be most disheartening for an athlete who, having set a record, finds it invalidated because of inaccuracies in the measuring.

Judging the Event

Judge 1 will be responsible for the conduct of the event. By operating out in the fan the judge will be in contact with the athletes and can keep the event moving. Competitors may commence jumping at any height above the minimum height, and may jump at their own discretion at any subsequent height. Three successive failures regardless of the height at which each failure occurs disqualify from further jumping. It is possible, therefore, for an athlete to have one or two failures at a particular height and decide to take the second or third attempts at a subsequent height.

While warm-ups are taking place, the judge should consult each athlete to determine their starting heights and to note their starting positions. High jumpers tend to wrap up warmly between jumps and numbers are not always visible. It certainly speeds the event along if the judge knows who to call and where to find them! It must be stressed that once a competitor passes a height, he or she cannot subsequently have a change of mind and attempt that height.

Unless otherwise stated on the programme, Judge 1 will be responsible for determining the starting heights and other heights at which the bar will be set. These shall be announced to the competitors before the start of the competition. The exception to this rule is when there is just one competitor left in the competition. The athlete is permitted to continue jumping until he or she has forfeited the right to continue and can, therefore, be consulted regarding subsequent height progression.

In jumping for height all recording on the cards should be as follows:

A successful jump	o
A failure	x
A jump not taken	–

Never leave a space empty (refer to the section on how to complete a height card).

Judge 2 and Judge 3 will operate from either side of the uprights and will be responsible for observing if any infringements take place at the take-off. They should position themselves in line with the plane of the uprights and will be responsible for setting the bar accurately at each height. It should be noted that if a record height is attempted, not only must it be carefully checked before the jump but also after as well if the height is cleared.

It shall be recorded as a failure if a competitor touches the ground or landing area beyond the plane of the uprights without having first cleared the bar. For example, an athlete aborts an attempt in the last stride or two and ducks under the bar making contact with the landing area, or runs past the uprights and in doing so touches the ground beyond the extended plane. Both would be recorded as failures.

An interesting point arises here. Most high jumpers these days adopt the 'Fosbury Flop' style of jumping. This style dictates that in the final stride of the approach run, the body is turned so that the athlete goes over the bar on his/her back. In arching the back, often the legs double up momentarily on take off, risking the possibility of brushing the landing area with a foot on the way up. The rule states that if contact is made and no material advantage is gained the jump should not be invalidated on this account. To compensate, this is the reason why there must be a minimum clearance of 10cm between the plane of the uprights and the landing area. This clearance should also prevent the bar being dislodged through any movement of the landing area during competition causing contact with the uprights.

Often a competitor touches the bar during a clearance and it wobbles precariously on the pegs. The judges must wait to see if any vibration set up will result in the bar falling from the pegs before they attempt to re-adjust it. They must be particularly observant on a windy day and be quite clear whether the bar fell as a result of the athlete knocking it or whether the wind was the true cause of it falling. If it was the latter, then the athlete will be given the benefit. If the wind sets up a vibration prior to the commencement of a jump, the bar should be steadied by the judges up to the last possible moment.

The use of time clock and, if possible, a wind sock is very important in jumping for height. It should be set up alongside the uprights in full view of the athletes and, of course, Judge 1. Each competitor needs to concentrate fully before attempting a trial — gauging the wind and the right conditions to take a jump. It is vital that they are aware of the time as jumpers often tend to use most of their allotted $1\frac{1}{2}$ minutes 'psyching' themselves up. Competitors who unreasonably delay making a trial and exceed the time limit render themselves liable to have that trial disallowed and recorded as a failure. For a second delay, at any time in the competition, they can be disqualified from taking further part in the competition. This is the equivalent of a disqualification on the track for two false starts. It is recommended that a T is placed over the x thus $\frac{T}{x}$, to denote a time fault. It must be recorded and, as it is commonplace for jumping for height competitions to last several hours, it will therefore be easy to recall previous time faults.

Although a number of different styles may be adopted — Fosbury Flop, scissors, straddle, etc — it is not permitted to take off from both feet. This is to prevent a somersaulting effect.

Once the judges are satisfied that an athlete has successfully cleared the bar without committing any infringements to the rules, it should be signalled by raising a white flag. A failure, for whatever reason, is indicated by raising a red flag.

New heights should always be announced and, if possible, displayed on a scoreboard for the benefit of athletes and spectators. The board should also show the competitor's number and the trial attempted. Unless there is only one competitor left, heights should never be raised by less than 2cms.

Check marks are permitted on the runway area to assist the athlete. Although there is no restriction on the number used under BAF rules, there is a maximum of two check marks only for competitions held under IAAF rules. It is recommended that adhesive tape or similar is used when check marks are necessary. Chalk, talcum powder and any other similar substances that leaves an indelible mark are not permitted. They are difficult to remove, and often the area can be covered in marks from previous competitions causing confusion to the athletes.

The situation sometimes arises regarding the athlete who is entered for more than one event and, after seeking permission from the judges, leaves the high jump to compete, for example, in a track race or another field event. The high jump competition continues and the athlete must rejoin it at whatever height the bar has reached. The bar is not lowered on his return to the height set at his departure.

As competitors are permitted to jump at their own discretion, High Jump and Pole Vault competitions tend to develop very much into tactical affairs. Competitions are often decided on countbacks and it is important that the judges familiarise themselves with the procedure for resolving ties which has been set out fully earlier in the book.

If an athlete, during a jump-off for first place, jumps a height higher than was achieved during the competition proper, this shall be recorded as the athlete's best height.

POLE VAULT

Duties of Officials

Judge 1 – Leader, card 1, height progression, call up, runway control, check spikes and numbers, time lapse, pole taping, validity of vault.

Judge 2 – Card 2, adjust stands, set bar, measure, plane of uprights, check scoreboard.

Judge 3 – Adjust stands, set bar, measure, pole plant, hands.

Safety Considerations and Preparation before the Start

Much of what was written for High Jump applies equally to Pole Vault. The wind is a critical factor with this event, largely due to the extra heights generated by the use of a pole. Any adverse wind can cause problems for vaulters, although they usually prefer a following rather than a headwind. At most stadia the pole vault equipment is usually set out by the ground staff well before officials and athletes arrive. It is important to check the wind direction and, if necessary, to consider changing the direction of jumping as early as possible to give time for this change to be made. If there is any doubt — for example, a tricky cross wind — there is nothing wrong in consulting the athletes. After all, they are the ones who have to jump!

The procedures for setting the bar are on similar lines to those for the high jump, except that the supporting pegs point away from the direction of run up.

Make certain that the stands can slide easily for the full distance permitted by the rules. The uprights should be positioned at zero for setting the bar, i.e. when the bar is vertically over the inside edge of the top of the stopboard. To accommodate the extra heights involved, the pegs are moved up and down by means of a winding mechanism on each upright. These are accurately graduated, and once the height of the bar has been checked and the verniers set and taped, the stands should lock out accurately each time the bar is raised. Care must be taken to wind each side up at the same rate to prevent the bar slipping off. A useful tip is for the judges to look at the opposite winder and keep pace with that. It will still be necessary to check any new height with an optical or other rigid measuring device.

It is not usual these days to provide vaulting poles. Athletes can use their own poles, and no one else can use a pole without the owner's consent. Glass fibre poles are very expensive and sophisticated now and are generally weight related to the individual vaulter. Occasionally at lower grade meetings, however, athletes are sometimes entered for a pole vault competition without possessing a pole of their own. On these occasions it is useful to see if there is a stadium all-purpose one available for general use.

It is useful to use a pole rack if one is available. It helps to keep the area tidy, and the poles can be easily covered when the conditions are wet.

Now that both men and women of all ages are permitted to participate in pole vault competitions, there is the likelihood that the bar will need

Deployment of Officials and Duties for Pole Vault

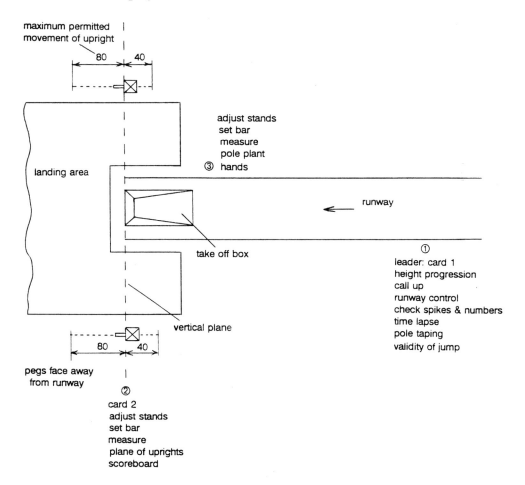

to be lowered below the normal limit of the stands which, in most cases, is around 2 metres. This will certainly be the case for the boys and girls in the younger age groups. It will be necessary to use purpose-made adaptors which fix rigidly to the uprights and give a lower position to place the bar. These fitments can then be removed once the height of the bar reaches that normally obtained by the stands.

Judging the Event

Judge 1 should operate down the runway and will be responsible for the smooth running of the event. By maintaining a close liaison with the athletes the judge can convey easily the jumping order to the vaulters, check that their numbers correspond to those on the card and see that any check marks are not on the runway but placed alongside it. This official will also operate the time clock. In pole vault each competitor has 2 minutes to complete the trial from the time the uprights and bar have been set.

It is possible for a vaulter to have the stands moved in either direction, but not more than 40cms from zero towards the runway (–40) or 80cms from zero away from the runway (+80). The athlete should inform the judges of his/her preference for the position of the uprights before the competition starts and this information should be noted on the card. This enables the judges to set the uprights according to each vaulter's wishes as soon as they are called. Any further adjustments made to the position of the uprights during the competition must be made before the bar is set and the time started.

Note: If the uprights have been moved from zero, the vertical plane always remains vertically over the top of the stop board. It is not the plane of the uprights.

The judge should also see that the poles conform to the rules regarding taping. Although poles can be of any length, diameter or smooth material, only two layers of tape are permitted for gripping purposes. Where tape is used it must provide a smooth surface without ridges, etc, which would give extra grip. Vaulters are sometimes seen replacing their adhesive tape during the competition and the judge must be observant to see that any replacement conforms to the rule and that an extra layer has not been added.

Judges 2 and 3 will operate at the take-off area, similar to the high jump. They will be responsible for adjusting the stands and setting the bar throughout the competition. One of the judges should note that, at the time of making a vault, the pole is correctly planted in the box and, after leaving the ground, the athlete does not place the lower hand above the other hand or move the higher hand further up the pole. This, in effect, would be climbing the pole to gain an advantage, which is not permitted.

The other judge should be positioned in line with the vertical plane. Provided the vaulter doesn't touch the ground or landing area beyond the vertical plane with any part of the body or pole, the trial can be started again (providing the 2 minutes time limit is not exceeded or the athlete has not infringed in any other way). This gives rise to an interesting point. Most landing areas are now manufactured to include projections on either side of the take-off box to protect the vaulter from injury. These projections are, in fact, in front of the vertical plane. No infringement would be incurred, therefore if, in the course of a trial, an athlete touched this part only of the landing area. It is suggested that a tape or similar line is positioned across the landing area to define the extent of the vertical plane.

When a vault is made, no one should touch the pole unless it is falling away from the bar or uprights. If it is touched and in the opinion of the judges or Referee it would have dislodged the bar from the pegs, it shall be recorded as a failure. At major competitions most competitors vault higher than the length of their poles so that the pole can easily pass under the bar without touching it. This is permissible, but the pole should still not be touched as it could possibly hit one of the uprights, dislodging the bar and resulting in a failure.

A point arises here when a commonsense interpretation of the 'spirit of the rules' should prevail. If, for example, an athlete is vaulting with a strong following or cross wind, it is quite possible that although the vaulter genuinely pushes the pole away on clearing the bar, the force of the wind blows it back. Under these exceptional conditions the officials should watch for this and catch the pole as it is pushed away.

On windy days it is often difficult to keep the bar firmly set on the pegs. On such occasions lengths of string tied to each side of the bar and held by the two judges would keep the bar steady until the last possible moment before the vaulter leaves the ground. It is important that the officials let the string go slack at this point. If they do not, it could prevent the bar falling off if it is hit by the vaulter; or, having cleared the bar, the pole could get caught on the string when it is pushed back, causing the bar to be dropped off.

If a pole breaks during the course of a trial it shall not be counted as a failure. Buckling or cracking would also be encompassed by the spirit of this rule.

When a competition is reduced to three or fewer competitors, under BAF rules the permitted time limit is increased to 4 minutes. For competitions held under IAAF rules, the time is further increased to 6 minutes when only one competitor is left. The time limit for consecutive trials by the same athlete, at any time during the competition, is 4 minutes from the moment the uprights are set.

The cards for pole vault should be kept as for high jump, i.e. o for a clearance, x for a failure, — for a jump not taken and Ⱦ for a time fault. The procedure for resolving ties is also the same.

THROWING EVENTS

SAFETY CONSIDERATIONS

It is absolutely vital that judges involved in these four disciplines display the utmost concentration at all times. The slightest lapse in attention, the quick glance at an exciting track race, trying to listen to results over the public address system or allowing one's attention to wander are all potential dangers. It is true to say that all aspects of judging demand each official to display a great deal of personal discipline, but never more so than judging in the sectors of the throwing events. Shot, discus, hammer and javelin involve potentially lethal implements, and the fact that there have been a number of fatalities and cases of serious injury only stresses the need to protect spectators, athletes and officials as much as possible.

To prevent unauthorised people wandering into the throwing areas during competition all sectors must be roped off. It is important also to stop people gathering in the danger areas outside the safety ropes. At some meetings photographers, keen to get pictures from different angles, are sometimes seen lying on the ground just outside the sector area. This is an extremely vulnerable position and it would be virtually impossible to move quickly should an implement stray off course. There shouldn't be any need whatsoever for anyone to be in this position.

The use of a safety cage is mandatory for throwing the hammer or discus. Either separate cages for each discipline or a combined cage for both is permissible. The cages must be so constructed and maintained as to prevent implements ricocheting or rebounding back at the athletes or over the top of the cage. The hammer cage must have two moveable panels or gates at the front, only one of which should be in operation at a time. Full specifications for safety cages are given in the current rule book.

The judges should inspect the appropriate cage and carry out any repairs or modifications before the event starts. Are there holes in the netting? Is the netting high enough? Can the gates move easily and be fastened in position? A hammer hitting an unfastened gate can cause the gate to swing and the hammer to ricochet anywhere. If repairs cannot be carried out, and in the opinion of the Referee and judges the cage is unsafe for the level of competition expected, they should give very careful consideration as to whether the event should proceed. It may be necessary, for example, to move the event to a less congested part of the programme or cancel altogether. It is better for all concerned to be safe rather than sorry.

Throwing implements must be under strict control at all times — both in warm up and in competition. Even though athletes are permitted to use their own implements (subject to checking), it is recommended that they are all returned to an appropriate rack and supervised by an official. At no time should competitors be allowed to wander around the area or competition site with implements. Regardless of their comments like "it's part of my warm up routine", "I only want to get a feel of the grip" or "I won't throw it" — they usually do!

All throws, including practice ones, must be made from the competition circle or arc and the implements must be returned by hand. This equally applies to officials as well as athletes. Do not, for example, roll back shot or discus. They can seriously damage an ankle of an unsuspecting athlete or official. One occasionally sees implements tossed to the side of the sector after a trial, ready to be carried back to the throwing area. This practice is also to be discouraged.

A competitor must not be called to commence a trial until it is clear that the judges and the measurement team in the sector are ready. It is recommended that the judge stands in the circle or on the runway until satisfied that the trial can begin. In hammer, discus and javelin events a warning horn should be sounded just before the athlete prepares to throw.

When judging the landing of an implement, the judges should stand on either side of the sector and converge to the point of landing. It is somewhat foolhardy to stand in the sector with the intention of being close to the point of landing. Discoi and javelin particularly are affected by the prevailing weather conditions and often drift in flight, while a hammer with its flailing handle is difficult to see. A judge who is trying to avoid an implement cannot be giving full attention to the exact point of landing.

In all long throws it is generally accepted practice to signal a no-throw by giving two blasts on the warning horn, as well as raising a red flag, for the benefit of the judges in the sector.

PUTTING THE SHOT

Duties of Officials

Judge 1 – Leader, card 1, call up, rear and front of circle, measure, time lapse.

Judge 2 – Card 2, front of circle, check measure, flags, supervise warm up.

Judge 3 – Rear of circle, arm action, tape through circle, implement control.

Judge 4 – Sector judge, spike, zero end of tape.

Deployment of Officials and Duties for Putting the Shot

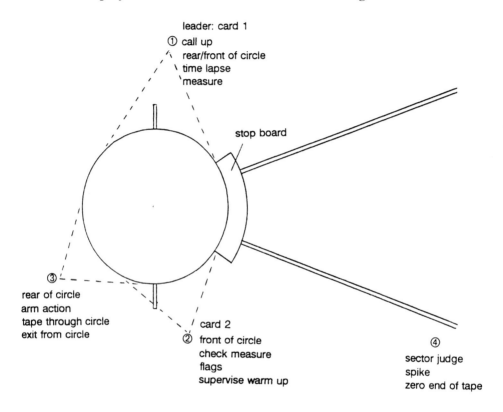

leader: card 1
① call up
rear/front of circle
time lapse
measure

stop board

③
rear of circle
arm action
tape through circle
exit from circle

card 2
② front of circle
check measure
flags
supervise warm up

④
sector judge
spike
zero end of tape

Safety Considerations and Preparation before the Start

Check that everything necessary to conduct the event is at hand. There should be a range of implements of the correct weight for the competition and, where possible, a rack for holding them. Sometimes a judging team have more than one shot event following consecutively. If different weights are involved, make certain that they are kept quite separately so that athletes do not use the wrong ones. It is not always possible to tell different weight shot just by their diameters!

Make certain that the stop board is firmly fixed down. Shot put is very much an explosive event, and the foot of the athlete will often exert considerable pressure on the front of the stop board as the implement is released.

There should be an ample supply of rags available for cleaning and drying the shot, a brush for sweeping the circle and, if the sector is a shale surface, a rake for smoothing the area is useful. A measuring tape and spike will be required, and where distance markers are supplied they should be checked to see that they have been positioned correctly.

Judging the Event

Judge 1 will be responsible for the control of the event. When the athletes arrive, confirm the order of putting and check that they are wearing two numbers as issued and that these correspond with the numbers on the card. On chilly days shot putters often keep a track suit or similar top on to keep their muscles warm. This is provided for in the rules, but when it occurs numbers must be worn on the outside. Check also for tape on the fingers. Gloves, pads, tapes, plasters or anything that could possibly assist an athlete to get extra grip or distance are not permitted. For example, the taping of two or more fingers together is against the spirit of the rules and cannot be accepted. The use of tape to cover injuries to the hand will only be allowed if the Referee is satisfied on medical grounds that the tape is necessary. Competitors are, however, permitted to use an adhesive substance — such as rosin — on their hands only to obtain a better grip. This is a difficult rule to apply strictly to the letter as it is obvious that once it is put on the hand it is automatically transferred to the implement as soon as it is handled.

A competitor must commence a trial from a stationary position in the circle. It is not permitted to enter the circle and in the same continuous movement discharge the implement. When a competitor begins a trial, it becomes a foul if any part of the body touches the top of the circle and/or the top of the stopboard or ground outside the circle. Touching the inside of the circle rim or stopboard is permitted. Often an athlete will commence the put from a crouching position, so that the shot moves up with the head to give extra impetus to the delivery. In this position the other hand hangs precariously close to the ground. The judge must note that this hand does not touch the top of the rim or ground outside.

A number of experienced shot putters have successfully developed a rotational movement across the circle similar to discus throwers. This is acceptable within the rules of competition, but as the shot circle is smaller than a discus circle, any lack of control in this confined space means that there is a real danger of the athlete fouling the circle or stopboard. Both officials must keep a careful watch for this as it happens very quickly.

The competitor must wait inside the circle until the implement has landed. This ensures that the athlete is completely under control and doesn't topple out as a direct result of being in an unstable position during the act of putting. When leaving the circle, the first contact with the top of the circle or ground outside the circle must be completely behind the white line which is drawn outside the circle.

Occasionally the concentration of a competitor is disturbed during a trial and the athlete may wish to stop and start the trial again. Provided that in the course of the trial the rules have not been infringed, the competitor can lay the implement down and may leave the circle before returning to commence a fresh trial. The time clock, however, is not restarted. Any interruption shall be included in the $1\frac{1}{2}$ minutes maximum time allowed for the trial.

Sometimes, after an implement has landed, athletes are disappointed with the distance and deliberately touch the top of the stopboard as a sign that they do not want it measured. This clearly invalidates the trial but it has been known

Leaving a Throwing Circle

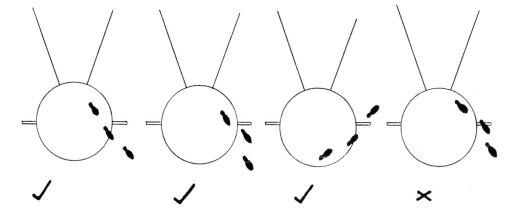

31

to cause some initial confusion to the inexperienced judge. It is important that the officials do not take their eyes off the circle until the athlete has left in a correct manner.

Judges 1 and 2 are also responsible for measuring and recording the distance putted after a successful trial. All measurements shall be recorded to the nearest centimetre below the distance covered, i.e. fractions of a centimetre should be ignored.

Although the shot is generally linked with the throwing events, it is technically not a throw at all, but a put. In fact if the shot is thrown it infringes the rules and must be recorded as a failure. The position of the shot prior to and during the act of putting is critical and must be watched very carefully. The rule is quite specific when it states that:

'The shot shall be put from the shoulder with one hand only. At the time the competitor takes a stance in the ring to commence a put, the shot shall touch or be in close contact with the chin and the hand shall not be dropped below this position during the act of putting. The shot must not be brought behind the line of the shoulders.'

Judge 3 must clearly see the position of the shot throughout the trial. In effect, this means that at the commencement of the put the shot should be held in close contact within the chin/jaw bone area until it is discharged. It should not be held behind the ear or back of the head as this is tantamount to being in a throwing position and therefore against the rules. At the moment the arm of the athlete goes into the delivery drive, the head and with it the chin straightens up and a gap will appear between the chin and the shot. At this stage the shot will not be in as close proximity to the chin as in the earlier stages of the put. This is not to be confused with the shot being taken away from the chin. The deciding factor must be the hand. If the shot is withdrawn in order to get extra drive, then the hand and with it the arm and elbow will move downwards and backwards. If the hand remains stationary than the delivery is a fair one.

The best position to observe this is from behind the circle with a clear view of the putting arm. The illustration showing the deployment of officials shows the position for a right-handed putter. A slight change of position will be needed if the athlete is left-handed.

After a successful put, Judge 3 will be responsible for correctly positioning the tape for measuring. It should be straight and must pass through the centre point of the circle. Judges 1 and 2 will measure the distance from the inside edge of the top of the stopboard. A white flag should be raised to indicate when a put is a valid one and red flag raised for a no-put.

Judge 4 is the sector judge marking the landing of the shot. The spike and zero end of the tape is placed at the edge of the indentation nearest to the circle. For it to be a valid put the implement must land completely within the inside edges of the 40 degree sector lines.

Although it is comparatively easy to see the mark made by the shot, continuous putting does considerably damage the ground and often a number of indentations are visible in a fairly confined area. The judge must carefully watch the flight of each trial, not only for safety but to make certain the correct indentation is marked.

THROWING THE HAMMER

Duties of Officials

Judge 1 – Leader, card 1, call up, rear and front of circle, warning horn, time, measure.

Judge 2 – Card 2, rear of circle, check measure, control implements, check gloves, exit from circle.

Judge 3 – Front of circle, tape through circle, supervise warm up, flags, set gates.

Judge 4 – Sector judge, spike, zero end of tape.

Judge 5 – Sector judge, spike, return implements.

Safety Considerations and Preparation before the Start

Throwing the hammer can be the most spectacular event and the most dangerous. It is vital that the officials arrive early at the site to check that the facilities are safe and to supervise all throws. Before all throwing events the attention of the competitors must be drawn to the rule that all throws — whether in practice or competition —

Deployment of Officials and Duties for Throwing the Hammer

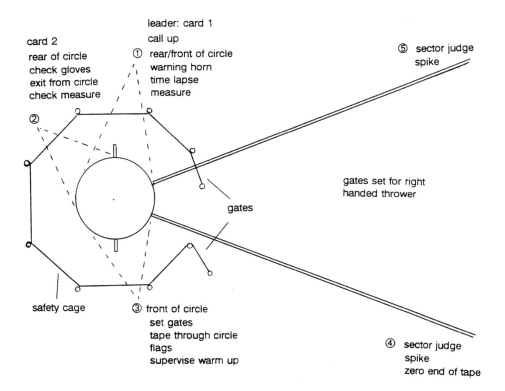

leader: card 1
call up
① rear/front of circle
warning horn
time lapse
measure

card 2
rear of circle
check gloves
exit from circle
check measure

②

⑤ sector judge
spike

gates set for right
handed thrower

gates

safety cage

③ front of circle
set gates
tape through circle
flags
supervise warm up

④ sector judge
spike
zero end of tape

must be from the circle only. This is particularly relevant in the hammer and must also apply to practice swings. The Referee is empowered to disqualify anyone who wilfully disregards these instructions after having their attention drawn to them.

Check that the safety sector is correctly roped off to prevent unauthorised people from entering the throwing sector during the competition.

Because of the severe friction caused by the hammer handle at the moment of release, hammer throwers are permitted to tape individual fingers and to wear gloves to protect their hands. These must be smooth front and back and the tips of the fingers must be exposed. This will permit the officials to check that fingers are not taped together. This would give the athlete a possible advantage and is therefore not permitted.

When not being thrown hammers should, wherever possible, be hung on an appropriate rack. Hammers lying around on the ground are easily damaged if the wires are trodden on — apart from being an obvious tripping hazard.

Make certain there are adequate rags for cleaning implements after each throw and a mat for athletes to wipe their feet before entering the circle, and that the necessary measuring tape, spike and flags are to hand to judge the event.

Judging the Event

Judge 1, as leader of the event, will be responsible for calling up the athletes to take their trials in the order stated on the card. This judge should also keep a check on the time allowed for each trial — 1½ minutes — and must sound the warning horn as the competitor enters the circle to commence the trial.

Judges 1, 2 and 3 should be positioned so that they can spot any infringements at the circle. The mandatory use of a safety cage can often give officials a false sense of security insomuch as there is the temptation to stand very close to the netting to carry out their duties. The speed at which a whirling hammer travels can extend the netting back at least a metre, sometimes more, and it would be impossible for the official to take the necessary evading action. There is no need for anyone to stand right up close to the netting to judge the event.

When a thrower enters the circle the trial must commence from a stationary position. The athlete may put the head of the hammer on the ground inside or outside the circle prior to starting, but at no time is the thrower permitted to touch the top of the metal rim forming the circle or the ground outside the circle.

Providing that in the course of a trial the rules have not been infringed, a competitor may interrupt a trial once started, may lay the hammer down and may even leave the circle before returning to a stationary position to start the trial again. This shall be done within the time limit allocated for the trial. However, if during the preliminary swings the head of the hammer touches the ground, whether inside or outside the circle, the athlete is not permitted to stop and start again. The phrase "stop throwing to begin the trial again" means that if the thrower stops turning and allows the head of the hammer to come to rest, either in the air or on the ground, then it is a fault and shall be recorded so. Should the hammer touch the ground during the preliminary swings and the athlete is able to stay in the circle and keep the rotation of the implement going, the competitor is permitted to complete the trial.

Occasionally when the hammer head hits the ground, the impact is sufficient to break the wire, causing the athlete to lose balance and foul the circle. If this happens a substitute trial is permitted. The appropriate rule states that if a hammer breaks during a throw or in the air, it shall not be counted as a trial — provided it was made in accordance with the rules. However, if a hammer breaks as a direct result of being thrown into the safety cage, so positioned as to restrain wayward implements, this would not be in the spirit of the rule and another trial should not be given.

To prevent hooking, the safety gates are designed to project partly into the throwing sector and appear to restrict the width of the cage opening. Inexperienced throwers sometimes find the use of them inhibiting, but any request to open the gate because it is offputting must be firmly rejected.

Due to the rotational delivery action, the wire handle continues to turn while the hammer is in flight. It sometimes happens that the handle — or even the hammer head — clips the cage on its way after being released. It should not, for this reason alone, be regarded as a foul. The cage is positioned for safety reasons and, provided no foul has been committed by the athlete at the circle and the first point of contact of the hammer with the ground is completely within the inside edges of the sector lines, it should be regarded as a valid trial. In reality, once the implement has made contact with the cage it will effectively lose some of its velocity, often resulting in a substandard throw. Be prepared for the competitor to deliberately foul the front of the circle by stepping out, indicating to the judges that he/she does not want it to be measured.

The sector judges will be responsible for marking the landing of the hammer in the sector. It is not essential to be close to the point of impact as the hammer will make a positive indentation in the ground. Even on very hard ground the mark will be clearly defined, but the judges must be alert to the possibility of the hammer bouncing. The wire handle also presents a hazard as it will still be rotating and is often difficult to see. On soft ground the hammer is often completely embedded. The judges should carefully remove the hammer without causing further damage to the ground and obliterating the mark to be measured. The spike and zero end of tape should then be positioned at the point of impact closest to the throwing circle, ready for the tape to be aligned through the centre of the circle. As in Throwing the Discus, all measurements must be taken from the inside of the metal rim of the circle and recorded to the nearest even centimetre below the distance covered if it is not a whole even centimetre. While the throw is being measured, judge 5 can remove the implement to the side of the sector or to the implement stand.

It is a good idea if the sector judges replace divots and repair the ground after each throw. A number of holes, caused by the hammer throughout the competition and during warm up, are likely to be spread over quite a wide area, and if a judge accidently puts a foot into one while moving in to measure, it could cause a fall or a twisted ankle.

Mention has already been made regarding particularly short throws and the possibility of athletes stepping out of the circle to indicate that they do not wish the throw to be measured. Never assume, however, that a short throw is going to be rejected by the thrower. Sometimes a competitor needs to record a throw — however short it is — to gain a point or to quality for further trials. The judges must be alert to every eventuality.

THROWING THE DISCUS

Duties of Officials

Judge 1 – Leader, card 1, call up, rear and front of circle, warning horn, time lapse, measure.

Judge 2 – Card 2, rear of circle, check measure, control implements, exit from circle.

Judge 3 – Front of circle, tape through circle, supervise warm up, flags.

Judge 4 – Sector judge, spike, zero end of tape.

Judge 5 – Sector judge, spike, return implements.

Deployment of Officials and Duties for Throwing the Discus

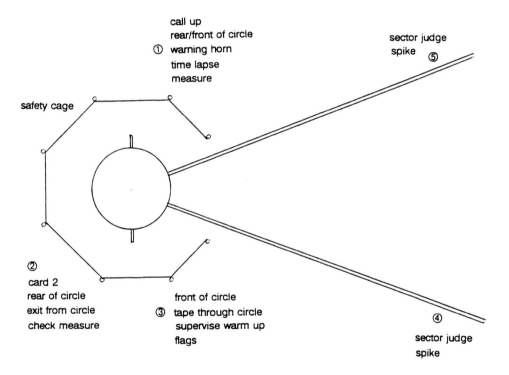

call up
rear/front of circle
① warning horn
time lapse
measure

sector judge
spike ⑤

safety cage

②
card 2
rear of circle
exit from circle
check measure

front of circle
③ tape through circle
supervise warm up
flags

④
sector judge
spike

Safety Considerations and Preparation before the Start

Discus is probably the most uncomplicated of all the throwing events. Providing the trial commences from a stationary position, an athlete is permitted to adopt any position or style and may make as many turns as necessary before releasing the discus.

Due to the speed generated by these turns there is a real danger of the discus being released in any direction, and it is mandatory that all throws, whether in practice or competition, must be made from a cage.

Due to the cost of installing safety cages, it is commonplace to see both hammer and discus competitions held from the same cage. Where this occurs several points must be taken into consideration.

(i) A discus cage does not use gates at the front. Check that the hammer gates are opened completely on both sides as far as they can go and bolted down securely — not just to clear the sector lines. The width of the cage opening is 6 metres and it should not be possible to see the gates when standing in the circle.

(ii) If the cage surrounds two separate circles, note that the discus is thrown from the larger one — set at the rear of the cage.

(iii) When the cage has concentric circles for hammer and discus, i.e. one circle 2.50 metres in diameter into which insets are fitted to reduce the diameter to 2.135 metres for throwing the hammer, remember to check the insets have been removed prior to a discus event.

As in all throwing events, it is necessary to see that there is an implement rack with an adequate supply of cloths to clean the implements, a brush to sweep the circle and a mat for competitors to wipe their feet on before entering the circle.

Judging the Event

Judge 1 should call up the competitors for their respective trials and must make certain that all officials and other athletes are outside the safety cage before allowing a trial to take place. When all is ready at the circle, a warning horn should be sounded to draw the attention of the sector judges and other competitors that a throw is due to commence.

The speed at which some competitors turn during a trial demands a great deal of concentration by the judges. It is often necessary to crouch down quite low to spot whether the circle has been fouled or not. As in judging the hammer, a wayward discus thrown into the cage will cause the netting to bulge considerably and it is important that the officials do not position themselves too close to the cage.

Judge 1 must see that the competitor starts the throw from a stationary position inside the circle, and doesn't touch the top of the circle or ground outside throughout the trial. Judge 2 will also watch for infringements at the rear of the circle, while Judge 3 should watch for any infringements on the other side of the circle, particularly at the front as the discus is released. By this method the three judges will be able to cover the complete circle eliminating any blindspots.

Judge 2 will also be in the ideal position to see that (a) the discus lands within the sector lines and (b) the athlete does not leave the circle until the implement has landed, and then by the correct method required by the rules.

If the trial has been a fair one, this should be signalled by raising a white flag, and a foul throw by a red one. It is suggested that two short blasts on the horn be given to indicate a no-throw to the sector judges.

Ideally, implement control in all throwing events should be carried out by a separate official who will only issue implements to the competitors as they are due to throw. Unfortunately, at the majority of meetings, there are rarely sufficient officials available to do this, so the task is usually incorporated with other duties amongst the judges at the circle.

Judges 4 and 5 are the sector judges and will mark the actual point of impact of the discus with the ground. They should be positioned on either side of the sector and, as they watch the flight of the discus, converge quickly to the point of landing. There are times when the mark is difficult to see, particularly when the ground is hard and the discus lands flat. Sometimes the only visible sign is a bruising of the grass. If the discus lands on its leading edge a curved mark will be clearly seen. Often, however, as the implement lands it makes two marks due to the spin imparted by the throwing action. On impact it will make a curved mark with the rear edge before tilting forward to make another bolder mark with the leading edge. It is from the rear mark, closest to the throwing circle, that the spike and zero end of tape are positioned for measurement. The judges therefore should not only get to the point of landing quickly, but also observe how it lands to find the correct mark.

A golden rule for all sector judges: keep your eyes on the implement throughout the trial and NEVER take your eyes off the point of impact for a moment. Better to mark it and then find out it was signalled a foul throw, than to glance up, assuming a no-throw, only to find a valid trial signalled and the mark is lost.

When measuring, a long tape is necessary. With the zero end and spike at the point of impact of the implement with the ground, the tape must pass through the centre of the circle in a straight line. The measurement is taken from the inside edge of the metal rim of the circle. The measurement recorded shall be to the nearest even centimetre below the distance covered, if that distance is not a whole even centimetre.

Although it is normal to have the tape extended throughout a competition so that measurements can be taken after each valid trial, it is important to make certain that the tape is under control at all times. It is suggested that the judge controlling the tape at the circle keeps the surplus wound in. When a throw is to be measured, the tape can be unwound as the judge walks to the circle and it can be lifted into position by the officials at both ends of the tape. Once the measurement has been taken and recorded, the surplus tape can be wound in and the tape lifted out of the sector as the judges resume their positions for the next trial. See the section on use and care of measuring tapes on page 46.

Where distance markers are used to indicate the best throw of each competitor, they are to be sited outside the sector lines. It helps the competition to flow smoothly if a separate official can carry out this task. A tape laid out along the sector line before the competition starts will enable the official to position the markers accurately.

THROWING THE JAVELIN

Duties of Officials

Judge 1 – Leader, card 1, call up, arc, warning horn, measure.

Judge 2 – Card 2, arc, flags, check measure, supervise warm up.

Judge 3 – Tape through 8m mark, arm action, time lapse, implement control, exit from runway.

Judge 4 – Validity of landing, flags.

Judge 5 – Sector judge, spike, zero end of tape.

Judge 6 – Sector judge, spike, return of implements.

Deployment of Officials and Duties for Throwing the Javelin

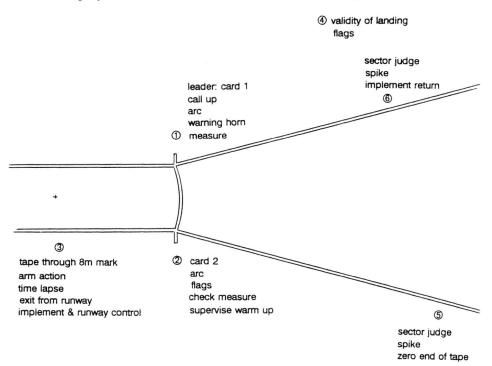

Safety Considerations and Preparation before the Start

As with all throwing events, it is important that the judges are at the competition site before the athletes arrive to ensure that safety measures are firmly enforced. When the athletes arrive there is a natural reaction for them to converge on the rack of javelins to select an implement for warming up. Remember that all warm up throws must be from the throwing arc and preceded by a signal on the warning horn — even at this stage when they are coming thick and fast. It is vital that the judges out in the field, assisting with implement return at this stage, be positioned outside the sector carefully watching each throw. Before the javelins are gathered up and returned to the arc it is essential for the judge leading the warm up to stand on the arc line in the centre of the runway to prevent any further throws taking place.

Another common practice during warm up is for throwers to place a javelin across their shoulders to stretch their upper body muscles by twisting and rotating. The judges must be particularly vigilant for this as it can be extremely dangerous in a crowded area.

Check that the safety ropes are correctly positioned. These should be at least 2m outside the sector lines and approximately 1m high. These ropes are designed to prevent unauthorised people from wandering into the throwing area from the sides. They will not prevent encroachment from the end of the sector. For competitions where 70m-90m throws are expected, it may be necessary to arrange for a further safety barrier across here if other events are taking place at the other end of the arena.

Before the competition starts, make certain that all implements are returned to the stand and are only issued as the athletes are called.

Check marks are not permitted on the runway or beyond the throwing arc. They are allowed, however, alongside the runway.

The javelin is truly a natural throwing event going back to early traditions of spear throwing. Although it has maintained its simplistic style, the modern javelin is far more sophisticated than its predecessors. Javelins are now aerodynamically designed and are often rated for distance as well. For example, a 70m rated javelin, designed to land correctly at around that distance, would not be a suitable implement for, say, an athlete only capable of throwing 30-40 metres. It would result in the javelin tending to land flat and, as this would be recorded as a failure, it would not be in the athlete's interest to use such an implement. It is important therefore to have a range of javelins in the pool to suit all competitors.

Judging the Event

Judges 1 and 2 should operate at the scratch line — one either side of the 8m radius throwing arc. They will be responsible for determining that no infringements occur as the javelin is released. It shall be recorded as a foul throw if a competitor touches the arc or the ground beyond the arc, including the extended scratch line, in the course of a trial.

The judges must resist any temptation to look up and follow the flight of the implement after it has been thrown. Fouls are most likely to occur at the moment of release or immediately afterwards, and it is vital that judges concentrate on the arc until the athletes have left the runway. Sometimes a thrower rotates forward after releasing the javelin, and the judges must be alert to the possibility of a hand or foot touching the ground on or beyond the arc to keep balance.

As in other throwing events, be aware of the competitor who, despite an apparently valid throw, deliberately steps beyond the scratch line as an indication that the throw is not to be measured. This act automatically invalidates the trial and it must be recorded as a no throw.

A competitor is not permitted to leave the runway until the implement has landed. This creates a problem for Judges 1 and 2 as it is virtually impossible on occasions to watch for infringements at the arc and to note when the javelin has landed. Judge 3, however, is in the perfect position to observe this. If this judge is positioned about 10-12 metres behind the arc alongside the

Over Shoulder or Upper Arm

runway, a clear view of the athlete, sector and javelin is obtained.

Judge 3 will also be in the best position to watch the arm action and to line the tape through the 8m mark when measuring a valid trial. The rules are quite precise with regard to how a javelin is held and thrown. It must be held with one hand only and at the grip so that the little finger is closest to the point. It must be thrown over the shoulder or upper part of the throwing arm. Any form of round arm action or hurling is not permitted, nor is any form of turning. An athlete is not allowed to turn completely round so that the back is towards the direction of throwing before discharging the javelin. The term "over the shoulder or upper arm" effectively means in the horizontal plane rather than the vertical, as illustrated.

Assuming the implement lands within the sector lines, the javelin is the only throwing event where, despite the athlete not committing any infringements at the throwing arc, it is possible for the throw to be adjudged a foul. Unlike Shot, Discus and Hammer, all of which are marked from the point of landing closest to the throwing circle, a valid throw in the javelin is dependent on how it lands. The rule states that a throw shall be valid only if the tip of the metal head strikes the ground before any other part of the javelin. Note it does not have to stick in, although it makes marking easier if it does. So a javelin that lands tail first must be recorded as a foul throw. So too must the implement that lands flat, with the grip being the first point of contact. In reality, judging the validity of landing has become such a critical factor as athletes strive for extra distance that a separate judge should be allocated to carry out this task. It is virtually impossible to combine judging validity of landing and spiking the point of contact with any degree of accuracy.

Judge 4 should stand well outside the sector lines so that a clear view is obtained of the javelin throughout its flight. The judge should try, whenever possible, to be positioned in line with the approximate point of landing. This will give the best opportunity of deciding whether the javelin has landed point first or not. From a distance it is possible to see quite clearly when the javelin is parallel to the ground on impact, or in the case of a valid landing, whether the point is lower then the tail. It will also be necessary, on occasions, to get down as low as possible to observe the landing. There have been many times when a javelin

looked certain to be landing flat, only for the point to dip at the last moment.

Once the judge is satisfied that the javelin has landed correctly in accordance with the rules, a white flag should be raised. If the implement lands flat or tail first a red flag should be raised. Flags must always be kept raised until acknowledged by the chief judge at the throwing arc.

Sector judges 5 and 6 should concentrate on marking the spot where the point of the javelin touched the ground first. They must converge from either side of the sector without taking their eyes off the mark. Under no circumstances must they pre-judge whether the javelin has landed flat. That is not their task. A judge that glances up on a marginal throw expecting to see a red flag has a problem if a white is raised. It is important that the sector judges converge quickly to the point of landing. It can certainly undermine an athlete's confidence in the officials if they amble out to the area where the implement landed and then proceed to hold a conversation as to where to put the spike!

As mentioned earlier, safety must be of prime importance when judging in the field. A javelin presents a very small profile in flight and can be difficult to see. This is particularly a problem at floodlit meetings and against crowded and multi-coloured backgrounds. Javelins, being light in weight, are very much affected by windy conditions and are easily blown off course. The judges must always make allowances for this. A judge who is trying to avoid a drifting javelin cannot be giving full consideration as to where it lands.

When measuring, the tape must be positioned by Judge 3 through the 8m mark on the runway. This is the centre of the radius of the throwing arc. All measurements must be taken from the inside edge of the arc by Judge 1, and recorded to the nearest even centimetre below the distance covered if the distance is not an even centimetre.

It is important to check that the tape is correctly aligned before the measurement is taken. See the paragraph in column two on page 36 regarding control of the tape, and also the section on the use and care of measuring tapes on page 46.

Once the event has finished and the cards completed, the judges must see that all throwing implements are removed from the competition site and returned to the Technical Manager or equipment store. In the interests of safety, implements must never be left unattended.

COMBINED EVENTS

Combined Events competitions involve a combination of disciplines from both Track and Field events. These competitions can be extremely demanding, but nevertheless form a tremendous challenge for the all-round athlete.

Although there is a range of combined event competitions to cater for indoors and for younger boys and girls age groups, the recognised outdoor combined events for record purposes are Heptathlon for women and Decathlon for men.

The Heptathlon consists of seven events which shall be held on two consecutive days of competition in the following order: Day 1 – 100 metres Hurdles, High Jump, Putting the Shot, 200 metres. Day 2 — Long Jump, Throwing the Javelin, 800 metres.

The Decathlon consists of ten events also held over two consecutive days of competition in the following order: Day 1 — 100 metres, Long Jump, Putting the Shot, High Jump, 400 metres. Day 2 — 110 metres Hurdles, Throwing the Discus, Pole Vault, Throwing the Javelin, 1500 metres.

Athletes compete in each of the disciplines and their best performances are related to points determined by the IAAF Combined Events scoring tables. The winner is the competitor who has achieved the highest number of points at the conclusion of the competition. In the event of a tie the winner shall be the competitor who has received the highest points in a majority of events. If this does not resolve the tie, the winner shall be the competitor who has scored the highest number of points in any one event. This procedure shall apply to ties for any place in the competition.

If an athlete fails to take part in any of the events it shall be considered that he or she has abandoned the competition. They shall not be permitted to take any further part in the competition and will not appear in the final result.

Normal competition rules will apply for each event with the following exceptions:

(a) In the Long Jump and each of the throwing events competitors shall be allowed three trials only.

(b) In track events, when hand timing is in operation, each competitor shall be timed by three timekeepers independently. Alternatively, times may be recorded by an approved fully automatic electronic timing device.

(c) In track events a competitor shall be disqualified in any event after three false starts.

(d) In jumping for height the bar shall be raised uniformly throughout the competition by 3cm in the High Jump and 10cm in the Pole Vault. The time allowed for a trial ($1\frac{1}{2}$ mins HJ, 2 mins PV) remains constant.

(e) In track events up to and including 200m and Long Jump the maximum permitted wind speed for record purposes must not exceed 4 metres per second.

The Combined Events Referee has jurisdiction over the conduct of a combined events competition. However, if Track and Field Referees are also appointed, they shall have jurisdiction over individual events within the competition.

If there are sufficient competitors to warrant dividing them into pools, it sometimes helps to divide them according to their high jump performance on the first day, and in the case of the Decathlon, their pole vault performances on the second day. Remember, however, it is one competition and each pool should have similar conditions. It would be unfair, for example, in the long jump if one pool jumped with the wind and the other pool jumped against it. If the conditions are not the same, then the second pool should commence immediately the first one has concluded.

It is not necessary for competitors to be in the same pools throughout the competition. It is quite common, for example, in the Decathlon to make up the javelin pools as the competitors are eliminated from the pole vault, providing there are sufficient to make up a pool, viz. at least a minimum of three. Prior to the final event, however, it must be determined who the leading competitors are as they all must compete in the same heat.

Whenever possible, there should be an interval of at least 30 minutes for each athlete between the time one event finishes and the next one begins.

At the conclusion of each individual discipline it is not necessary to complete the result cards by placing the athletes in finishing order. All that is required is for the competitors best trial to be carried forward to the final column. These will be converted into points from the scoring tables by the Referee and/or Recorders. Note: scoring no points is not the same as failing to take part in an event.

WEIGHTS OF FIELD EVENT IMPLEMENTS

Group	Age	Discus	Shot	Javelin	Hammer
U13 Boys	11 & 12	1.00 kg	3.25 kg	400 g	N/A
U15 Boys	13 & 14	1.25 kg	4.00 kg	600 g	4.00 kg
U17 Men	15 & 16	1.50 kg	5.00 kg	700 g	5.00 kg
Junior Men	17 to 19	1.75 kg	6.25 kg	800 g	6.25 kg
Senior Men	20 & over	2.00 kg	7.26 kg	800 g	7.26 kg
Men Vets.	40 to 49	2.00 kg	7.26 kg	800 g	7.26 kg
	50 to 59	1.50 kg	6.00 kg	800 g	6.00 kg
	60 to 69	1.00 kg	5.00 kg	600 g	5.00 kg
	70 & over	1.00 kg	4.00 kg	600 g	4.00 kg
U13 Girls	11 & 12	0.75 kg	2.72 kg	400 g	N/A
U15 Girls	13 & 14	1.00 kg	3.25 kg	600 g	N/A
U17 Women	15 & 16	1.00 kg	4.00 kg	600 g	4.00 kg
Junior Women	17 to 19	1.00 kg	4.00 kg	600 g	4.00 kg
Senior Women	20 & over	1.00 kg	4.00 kg	600 g	4.00 kg
Women Vets.	35 to 49	1.00 kg	4.00 kg	600 g	4.00 kg
	50 & over	1.00 kg	3.00 kg	400 g	3.00 kg

It is recommended that implements issued for competition under BAF rules should exceed the specified weights by at least 5 g.

For competitions held under IAAF rules implements should exceed the specified weights by 5 g but not exceeding 25 g.

Complete specifications of all implements can be found in the current BAF/IAAF Rulebooks.

ELECTRONIC DIGITAL MEASUREMENT (EDM)

The use of EDM for measuring is now standard practice for International, Championship and National events. Although, in the initial stages of its development, the system was used mainly for measuring long throws, it is now used on all events including horizontal and vertical jumps.

As the equipment becomes more widely available its use will eventually spread to a variety of other meetings. This, in turn, will require a greater number of officials to be familiar with and experienced in setting up the equipment and understanding the method of operation.

In principle it operates in a similar manner as a theodolite linked to a computer. The EDM unit must be set on a tripod with a clear view of the event site. Prior to the start of an event the EDM will be set and checked for accuracy using a steel tape.

For throwing events this requires a prism to be positioned in the centre of the throwing circle —

or the 8m point in the case of javelin. By focusing on the prism the unit records and stores the distance in the computer (x on the diagram). It will also store the radius of the appropriate circle or arc.

When an implement is thrown, the sector judge uses the prism spike to mark the point of impact in the normal way, pointing it towards the EDM unit. This is focused on the prism and it measures and records the distance (y on the diagram). Once both distances x and y are recorded, the computer automatically calculates the included angle and, by the process of triangulation, the third side of the triangle. It then subtracts the appropriate radius and also rounds down to the next centimetre or next even centimetre as appropriate. The measurement is recorded both on a digital read-out and a computer printout and can also be linked to an electronic scoreboard.

In jumping for distance and height, the principle is exactly the same except that the measure-

Electronic Digital Measurement (EDM)

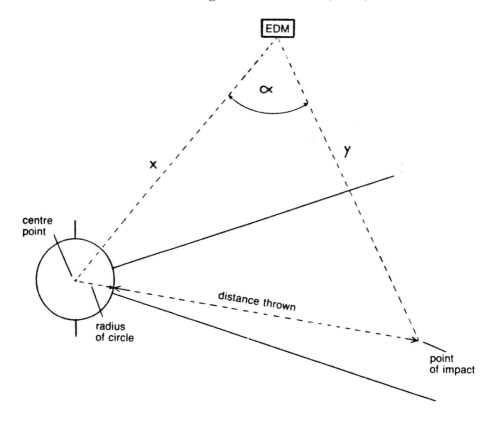

ments are taken from a standard baseline rather than from a circle point.

When EDM is in operation, it is usual practice for Card 1 to be kept by the appointed official at the EDM unit. Card 2 would be kept by an official at the scoreboard if a manual board is in operation. It is not necessary for the officials judging the event to wait for a distance to be displayed before calling up the next athlete. Once the EDM operator has signalled to the judge with the prism spike that the measurement has been recorded, the prism can be removed and the next athlete called up while the computer is calculating the distance. It is recommended that cards used by the judges on call up should be confined to just a tick when the athlete has taken the trial. This procedure helps the event to flow smoothly and efficiently.

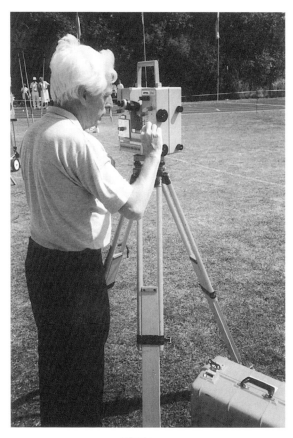

EDM in use

PRODUCING AND USING A DUTIES LIST

There are many different duties undertaken by officials in the course of judging field events — over 30 when all 8 events are taken into consideration.

As officials gain experience and judge regularly, most or all of these duties will be carried out over a period of time. Some officials develop an interest in only one or two events for a variety of reasons and clearly become quite proficient in these events. However, when seeking upgrading to a higher level, officials would be expected to show that they have gained experience and a good understanding of all eight events.

It is now common practice for Referees, whenever possible, to produce a duties list prior to a meeting to hand out to the judges as they arrive. It is not only useful for inexperienced officials to know exactly their duties before the start of an event, but this is also good practice and enables a competition to flow smoothly and efficiently by encouraging team work. An example of the typical deployment of officials and their duties is given at the commencement of each discipline earlier in the book.

Before producing a duties list, it is important to obtain a programme and timetable of events and a list of officials with their grades well in advance of the meeting. It is helpful to know if enough officials have been appointed to man all events safely, or whether you need to try and get extra help. This saves a lot of hassle if it can be resolved before the day of the meeting. It is sometimes useful if some of the officials are known to you. It is then possible to allocate officials according to strengths and experience, enabling each judging team to have a balance of officials. At some meetings this may also enable a judge to observe and write a report on a lower graded official in preparation for future upgrading.

A typical strategy for the preparation of a duties list is given next.

A Suggested Strategy for Producing a Duties List

Stage 1: Before you start, consider:
— Timetable
— What events are there?
— Type of meeting
— Number of competitors/events
— How long is each event likely to last?
— Number of officials (a) graded, (b) others

Stage 2: Timing of events — all throws and horizontal jumps

* An event with 8 competitors each with 6 trials = 48 trials
thus, $48 \times 1\frac{1}{2}$ mins = 72 mins

however, taking into consideration:

(a) a proportion of no jumps or throws

(b) throws will be quicker than jumps — no raking required
the approximate time for a Throws event would be 55-65 mins and for horizontal Jumps approx 65-75 mins.

* Remember, it is essential to have an experienced call up judge if at all possible.

HIGH JUMP AND POLE VAULT

* A good yardstick for these events is to work on an average of 7 trials per competitor and multiply by 2 for HJ and $2\frac{1}{2}$ for PV.

Thus:	High Jump	Pole Vault
	8 competitors $\times$ 7 = 56 trials	8 $\times$ 7 = 56
	56 $\times$ 2 mins = 112 mins approx	56 $\times$ $2\frac{1}{2}$ = 140 mins approx

* This includes putting on bars, moving uprights, straightening beds etc.

continued on next page

Stage 3: Tabulate start and finish time per event

* Remember to allocate adequate time for warm-up for each event.

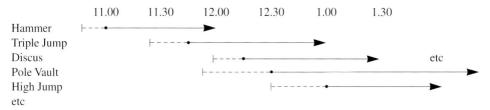

	11.00	11.30	12.00	12.30	1.00	1.30
Hammer						
Triple Jump						
Discus						etc
Pole Vault						
High Jump						
etc						

Stage 4: List key duties per event

* You may consider, for example, that Javelin has 3 key positions:
  validity of landing, spike, throwing arc.
  Other events, maybe, have only 1 or 2.

* Remember, it is easier to spike in Hammer or Shot than Discus.

* Appoint key positions first.

* Balance your teams with experienced and less experienced officials.

* If you are short of officials or several are likely not to turn up, bear in mind the MINIMUM number
  to run each event. (Actual deployment can only be done on the day when you know the situation)
  e.g. HJ 2, PV 2, Shot 3, etc.

Stage 5: Tabulate events with officials on a simple grid

Events Officials & Grade	11.00 Hammer	11.45 Triple Jump	12.15 Discus	12.30 Pole Vault	1.00
A 1				I/C	
B 2	I/C				
C 2		✓			
D 3	✓				
E 3				✓	
etc			✓		

Stage 6: Finally allocate duties and produce a complete duties sheet

USE AND CARE OF MEASURING TAPES

When using measuring tapes it is important that judges do not allow them to become damaged by careless handling. While it is reasonable to expect a tape to be extended throughout a competition, the judges should keep the surplus tape fully wound in and not just strewn around the circle or take off area. Apart from being visually untidy, it can create a safety hazard that can trip an athlete or official and it can be irreparably damaged if trodden on. When kinks occur — particularly on steel tapes — it usually results in breakage within a short time.

As mentioned earlier in the book, the judges on both ends of the tape should lift the tape into position when taking a measurement and lift it out again afterwards. It should never be dragged along the ground as this results in the tape coiling up. This inevitably gives an inaccurate reading, particularly over longer distances.

Although the majority of measuring tapes are manufactured with zero starting from the outside of the metal loop, this is not always so. It is advisable to check all tapes for accuracy before the start of a competition. A simple check on glass fibre tapes is to fold the tape at, say, the 50 cm mark and if the measurement is from the outside of the loop it should be level with the 1m mark.

The alternative is to use another tape as a check. It is not recommended to fold a steel tape.

When measuring it is probably easier to put the spike through the loop and use the spike and tape as one unit. Remember, however, to allow for the thickness of the metal loop. The alternative is to put the spike in at the mark to be measured and hold the end of the tape against the spike. Whichever method is adopted, care must be taken to see that the zero point of the tape is positioned in the correct place. The judge pulling the tape through at the circle or scratch line must not pull too hard. This can result in a loss of distance if the spike is pulled over or the metal loop pulled away from the spike. It is often useful, over longer distances, for the spiker to put a foot on the tape to prevent this happening.

The judges reading the measurement must avoid the temptation to try to assist in straightening or aligning the tape. This usually results in a "dog leg" effect in the tape. This is a common occurance, especially in the javelin event, when the official is trying to position the tape through the 8m mark. This official is solely responsible for aligning the tape correctly before a measurement is taken.

How to Measure

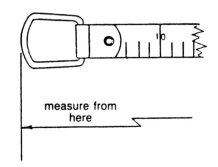

measure from here

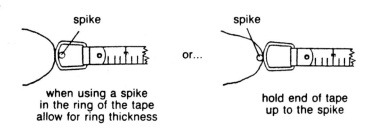

spike

when using a spike in the ring of the tape allow for ring thickness

or...

spike

hold end of tape up to the spike

ESSENTIAL EQUIPMENT FOR FIELD JUDGES

(1) Current rule book — important to keep up to date with rule changes.

(2) Clip board or all weather writer — to take the event card.

(3) Clear polythene bag to cover the card in wet weather.

(4) Pencils and pens — preferably ones that write under all conditions.

(5) Eraser — we all make mistakes some time!

(6) Waterproof clothing — a must in this country.

(7) Spike and tape — for measuring performances.

(8) Coloured adhesive tape — useful for check marks, etc.

(9) Safety pins — running repairs with numbers during competition.

The good judge, however, will be constantly adding to this list as he or she gains experience.

Warning horn — for safety use on long throws.

Trowel and wallpaper roller — for repairing no-jump indicator.

Callipers — for checking diameters, Shot, Discus, etc.

Spanners and screwdriver — emergency repairs to faulty equipment, etc.

Finally, a suitably sized holdall will be necessary to carry the equipment, bearing in mind that the current rules state that no form of advertising is to be taken into the arena other than approved sponsorship contracts. This includes holdalls.

QUALITIES REQUIRED OF A FIELD JUDGE

A thorough knowledge and understanding of the rules for competition.

Good powers of concentration.

Tact.

Quick reactions.

Common sense.

Decisive but pleasant manner.

Ability to get on with other officials.

Meticulous care in measuring and recording.

Finally, a thorough understanding of the needs of an athlete and the requirements of the competition.

TESTING AND GRADING OF FIELD OFFICIALS

The British Athletic Federation operates a scheme for testing and grading of officials within the United Kingdom. Officials may become qualified in one or more categories: Track, Field, Timekeeper and Starter/Marksman. Each discipline is administered by the BAF Officials Committee through Regional, District, County and Service Associations.

Grade 4 This is the initial grade which is obtained by passing the preliminary written paper — the pass mark of which is 65%. Candidates are expected to have a good grasp of the main rules for competition and to have had some practical experience. Tests are usually held following a series of instructional sessions by senior officials.

Grade 3 County Level
For promotion to Grade 3 an official must have had at least 1 years experience as a Grade 4 and have been given at least one satisfactory report by an experienced higher graded official. A list of meetings and duties undertaken by the official must be received before upgrading can be approved.

Lists of officials within Grade 4 and Grade 3 are maintained by County/District/Service Associations.

Grade 2 Area Level
For promotion to Grade 2 an official must have had considerable experience as a Grade 3 judge for a minimum of 2 years and have received at least two good reports from different higher graded officials. A record of meetings and duties undertaken during the previous 2 years must also be submitted. Upgrading in the minimum time will only be accorded to the outstanding candidate as determined by the quality of the reports and the scope and range of duties covered.

Lists of officials within Grade 2 are maintained by Regional and National Associations.

Grade 1 International Level
For promotion to Grade 1 an official must have had considerable experience for at least 3 years as a Grade 2 judge. The duties lists should indicate a range of meetings and duties of an appropriate high standard. In addition an advanced test must be successfully completed, the pass mark of which is 75%. Invitation to take the advanced test will be made by the appropriate Regional or National Association. A minimum of three good reports from experienced and active higher graded officials must be received. A successful candidate is also expected to have experience (and preferably a satisfactory report) as a Clerk of the Course — Field.

The list of officials within Grade 1 is maintained by the BAF National Officials Committee and forms the basis for selection for National and International meetings within the United Kingdom.

Grade 1 (Referee) International Level
Officials from within Grade 1 may be invited to become Grade 1 Referees provided they have:

(a) At least 3 years extensive experience within Grade 1 including National and International meetings as a judge.

(b) Considerable experience as a Referee at Regional Championships and meetings of similar standard.

(c) Excellent written reports on the candidate operating as a Referee from at least three active Referees.

Full details of the syllabus for the preliminary and advanced tests together with additional information regarding the Grading Scheme for Officials can be found in the current BAF Handbook.

APPLICATION FOR A RECORD

It is important that field officials are aware of the procedures to be adopted when a record is established. The only records officially recognised are those for Senior and Junior (U20) men and women, while the accepted field events are those for which the IAAF recognise world records. These currently are:

Outdoors — Long Jump, Triple Jump, High Jump, Pole Vault, Shot Put, Discus, Hammer and Javelin with Decathlon for men and Heptathlon for women.

Indoors — Long Jump, Triple Jump, High Jump, Pole Vault and Shot Put with Heptathlon for men and Pentathlon for women.

For Junior records in throws events, all performances must have used implements conforming to senior specifications.

A record form does not have to be completed for other events or age groups. These are regarded as best performances although it is useful to pass on any performances for statistical purposes.

The event should have a minimum of three competitors taking part. The distance or height must be measured by three judges — including the Referee — using a steel tape or bar, or alternatively a suitably approved scientific measuring device. In the case of High Jump and Pole Vault, not only should the height be checked before the attempt but also after the height has been cleared.

For outdoor record claims in Long and Triple Jump, information regarding wind conditions must be available. A wind gauge must be set up correctly and any following wind must not exceed 2 metres/sec (or 4 metres/sec in the case of a combined event).

If a record is claimed in a throwing event, the implement should be checked and re-weighed immediately, NOT at the end of the competition. It can then be returned to the competition pool.

If a National (including English, Scottish, Welsh and Northern Irish), United Kingdom All-Comers' or Commonwealth record is equalled or bettered, then the standard U.K. form should be completed. A copy of this is shown on page 50. The completed form, with a copy of the programme for the meeting and an official results list, should be sent to the Honorary Secretary of the BAF.

If a foreign athlete establishes a National record and requires documentation to support this, a standard U.K. form could be used, but the form shown on page 51 has been specially designed for this purpose and requires only two signatures, that of the Referee and of a representative of the National Association, to verify the qualifications of the officials concerned and the status of the stadium facilities.

For World or European records a similar procedure is adopted except that the appropriate IAAF World record form must be completed.

British Athletic Federation

U.K. All-Comers   U.K. National   U.K. Junior   Other record (please specify)..
(Reference should be made to B.A.F. Rule 141 : I.A.A.F. Rule 148)

1.	Event...Indoors/Outdoor	2.	Date.........................
3.	Performance...	4.	Meeting..............................
5.	Venue...	6.	Wind Reading..................................
7.	Name of competitor...		

<table>
<tr><td></td><td>First Name</td><td></td><td>Surname</td></tr>
</table>

8.   Date of Birth.....................................   9.   Place of Birth.....................................

10.   Club/Country...

For Relay Events details are required of the team in running order:-
1...   2..
3...   4..

TIMEKEEPERS' CERTIFICATE

Complete section 1 or 2 as appropriate:

1.   A fully automatic, correctly aligned, electrical timing device, was used. I confirm the time above.

Name of Photo-finish Chief...Signature..
or

2.   We certify that we were official timekeepers of the above event and that the exact time recorded on our watches for the competitor concerned was:

Time	Signature	Name	Grade

I confirm that the official time for the competitor named was...

Name of Chief Timekeeper...Signature....................................Grade.................................

STARTER'S CERTIFICATE

I certify that the start of the race was in accordance with the relevant Rules.

Name of Starter...Signature....................................Grade.................................

WALKING JUDGE'S CERTIFICATE

I certify that I was Chief Judge of Walking for the above event and that the competitor concerned complied with the definition of walking under B.A.F./I.A.A.F. Rules and that this was confirmed by three suitably qualified Judges of Walking.

Name of Chief Judge..Signature....................................Grade.................................

DOPING CONTROL CERTIFICATE

(Not necessary for U.K. All-Comers Records unless performance is also U.K. National, European or World Record)
I certify that the above mentioned competitor(s) provided a sample for drug testing in accordance with Rule 24 and Appendix B of the B.A.F. Rules for Competition.

Name of Official...Signature..
Status..

REFEREE'S CERTIFICATE

I certify that all the conditions as laid down by B.A.F./I.A.A.F. Rules for Competition were complied with and that the performance was made in bona fide competition in accordance with these Rules. The following information is attached:-
1.   A schedule giving lap times and the name of the leader for each lap.
2.   A copy of the photo-finish picture.
3.   A copy of the Field Event scorecard which shows the grade of the officials for the event.
4.   A copy of the programme of the meeting.

Name of Referee..Signature....................................Grade.................................

British Athletic Federation

RECORD OF PERFORMANCE

Event . . . .   Meeting . . . .

Performance . . . .

Venue . . . .   Date . . . .

Wind-speed and direction . . . .

Competitor's name (BLOCK CAPITALS) . . . .
(First Names)   (Surname)

For relay events, please enter the name of the team above and the names of the athletes below, **in the order of running**:

(1) . . . .

(2) . . . .

(3) . . . .

(4) . . . .

PHOTO/SCORE CARD ENCLOSED

Referee's Certificate

I certify that the performance claimed was achieved in bona-fide competition held in accordance with I.A.A.F. Rules. The Judges and Officials controlling the event were properly qualified and approved by my National Association. The equipment used was verified and conforms with I.A.A.F. Specifications.

Signature of Referee . . . .

Certificate of National Association

As the authorised representative of the . . . .
I certify that the statements recorded above are fully authentic.

The stadium facilities (track, runways, throwing-circles and landing areas) have been properly surveyed, and conform with I.A.A.F. specifications in all respects.

Signed . . . .   Date . . . .